PUFFIN BOOKS

# THE AMAZING WORLD OF PLANTS

Have you heard of the bladders of doom? Do you know about rocket-propelled cucumbers? Have you ever seen a living stone? How do pongy plants attract insects?

Phil Gates has all the answers and he has made sure that they are in this book. You'll also be able to find out how the first plant appeared millions of years ago and how human beings depend on plants in so many ways. Topics such as plant reproduction, the different plant species, plant explorers, the world's most poisonous plants, plant perfumes, plant treasure, and plant magic and medicine are all dealt with and explained in a lively, interesting and understandable way.

Read the book the whole way through, or dip into it using the contents and index pages. The glossary will explain any new scientific word you may not have come across before. There are experiments to do, factfiles to remember, plant horror stories to tell your friends and much more besides in this PLANTASTIC information book.

Phil Gates is a lecturer in Botany at Durham University. He specializes in making science fun and writes regularly for the *Independent on Sunday* and the *Guardian*, on botanical matters. He lives in Crook, Co. Durham, with his wife and three children. His first book for children, *The Aliens are Coming*, is also published in Puffin.

*Also by Phil Gates*
The Aliens are Coming

# The Amazing World of Plants

. . . . . . . . . . . . . . . . . . . . . . . .

## PHIL GATES

### ILLUSTRATED BY JULIA CASSELS

PUFFIN BOOKS

PUFFIN BOOKS

Published by the Penguin Group
Penguin Books Ltd, 27 Wrights Lane, London W8 5TZ, England
Penguin Books USA Inc., 375 Hudson Street, New York, New York 10014, USA
Penguin Books Australia Ltd, Ringwood, Victoria, Australia
Penguin Books Canada Ltd, 10 Alcorn Avenue, Toronto, Canada M4V 3B2
Penguin Books (NZ) Ltd, 182–190 Wairau Road, Auckland 10, New Zealand

Penguin Books Ltd, Registered Offices: Harmondsworth, Middlesex, England

First published 1993
10 9 8 7 6 5 4 3 2 1

Typeset by Datix International Limited, Bungay, Suffolk
Printed in England by Clays Ltd, St Ives plc

# CONTENTS

# 1

. . . . . . . . . . . . . . . . . . . . . . . . .

# HAVE YOU USED A PLANT TODAY?

Read through this checklist. Tick the boxes if you have used any of the items listed today.

- **Food**

Grass seeds (cereals, bread) □

Other seeds (baked beans, peas, coffee, chocolate) □

Leaves (tea, vegetables) □

Roots (carrots, beetroot) □

Spices (sauces) □

Tropical fruits (bananas, pineapples, oranges) □

Crystallized plant sap (sugar) □

Fats and oils from plants (margarine and cooking oil) □

Flavourings from plants (sweets, most foods, toothpaste) □

Meat and milk (from farm animals fed on plant products) □

Seaweed extracts (in many sauces and preserved foods) □

Plant sap (fruit juices) □

- **Clothing**

Hairs from the outside of seeds (cotton clothing) □

Rubber (soles of shoes) □

- **Medicine**
Forty per cent of medicines from chemists,
including things like cough mixtures and ointments,
contain plant extracts ☐

- **Housing**
Wood (floor-boards, roof beams) ☐

- **Entertainment**
Wood pulp (newspapers, books, magazines) ☐
Wood (musical instruments, eg guitars, violins) ☐

- **Consumer goods**
Perfumes (scents, shampoos, deodorants, soaps) ☐
Wood (furniture) ☐

- **Travel**
Rubber (car, bus and bicycle tyres) ☐
Fossil fuels (oil) ☐

- **Energy**
Heat and light from fossil fuels (oil, gas, coal) ☐

- **Sport**
Grasses (playing fields) ☐
Wood (bats, snooker cues, goal-posts) ☐
Rubber (shoes and balls) ☐

You will probably find that you can tick almost all the boxes. That is why plants are so important. Your whole life depends on them. Where did they come from? And how and why are there so many different plants? Read on and all will be revealed! Words in bold are explained in the glossary.

# 2

· · · · · · · · · · · · · · · · · · · · · · · · ·

# THE DEATH OF A STAR

It all began with a mighty bang. Somewhere in the depths of space a star exploded. In the inky blackness a vast, swirling cloud of dust and gases was created.

**Gravity** pulled these together into the centre, until they became a huge ball of superhot gases, rocked by thermo-nuclear explosions and radiating intense energy. This was the birth of the sun.

The dust specks that orbited the sun collided and stuck together, growing into ever-larger rocks. They tumbled and span and smashed into one another in a whirling merry-go-round of destruction. As they grew their gravity increased, attracting smaller rocks that plunged into their surface. A few grew larger than the others and became the planets. One of these was ours.

## ● The birth of the earth

After this violent beginning, 4,500 million years ago, the earth orbited the sun as a dead planet. From time to time giant meteorites collided with its surface and the heat of the collisions produced seas of molten larva. Meanwhile, in the core of the earth, **radioactive** elements decayed, creating white heat that turned the heart of the planet into a mass of boiling, molten rock, which in turn belched to the surface in volcanoes. Evil-smelling, poisonous gases poured out of these vents in the earth's fiery core.

Slowly the collisions with meteorites became rarer and the surface began to cool. Billowing clouds formed, shielding the surface from the sun's intense heat, and rain began to fall. Somewhere, perhaps in a rock-pool on the edge of an ocean, life began.

● **The living planet**

To begin with there was no **oxygen** in the atmosphere, so it smelled of rotten eggs. The first living things probably survived on **sulphur**. They were microscopic and grew in enormous numbers in the soupy waters of the oceans. Then, perhaps four thousand million years ago, a microbe appeared that was green – the first plant.

The green colour came from a substance called **chlorophyll**, which had the amazing property of trapping energy from sunlight. The microbes used this to make sugars from water and carbon dioxide, in a process called **photosynthesis**. They used the sugars for food and growth. Most importantly of all, they released oxygen as a waste product.

The atmosphere contained unlimited quantities of **carbon dioxide** and water, and the sun provided all the energy that these primitive plants could need. So they multiplied rapidly, giving off more and more oxygen and creating an atmosphere identical to that which we breath today.

You and I are here because of that tiny green **bacterium** which evolved somewhere in the earth's seas all those millions of years ago.

● **Invading the land**

The length of time that has passed since the earth formed

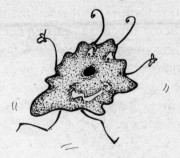

is so great that it is beyond the power of the imagination of puny humans, who live on average for about seventy years.

For thousands of millions of years life continued to evolve in the sea. The microscopic plant **cells** multiplied and grew larger, some forming into seaweeds. Worms, shellfish, and fish evolved too, feeding on plants and on each other.

Life was richest around the warm, shallow waters of the coast. Every day tides rose and fell, leaving plants high and dry for hours at a time. Slowly their leafy fronds grew tougher, so they were able to store water and not be killed by the heat of the sun. They also developed roots that could grow downwards to reach the water below.

The first plants to invade land were probably primitive **liverworts.** They were mostly tiny, fragile plants that grew in the shade and depended for survival on regular rainfall and moist conditions. Other tougher plants, with strong stems and deep roots, also developed.

First came ferns, some in shapes and forms that we would still recognize today. Some grew into giant trees

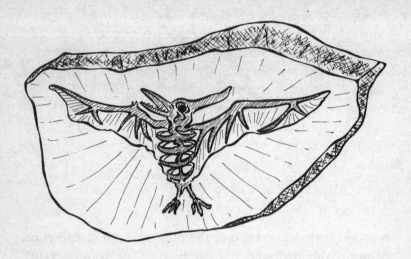

and formed dense, dripping forests where the colours were mostly greens and browns. By this time animals had also invaded the land. Amphibians slithered in the swamps and the first dinosaurs roamed the earth.

### ● Disaster strikes

The dinosaurs might still be here today, if it had not been for a giant wandering meteorite that appeared from outer space and struck our planet. The impact was devastating. Life was destroyed over a wide area. Dust thrown into the atmosphere blotted out the sun and the earth became as cold as winter. Dinosaurs and many other animals and plants were exterminated. We only know that they existed from the fossils they left behind.

But when the dust cleared and the sun shone again, new types of animals and plants arose. The ancestors of pine trees appeared. Birds and mammals replaced the dinosaurs. And then new colours began to appear. In the green, clammy, tropical jungles flowers opened. The air hummed with insects.

Flowers produced seeds that could survive long periods of drought. Primitive ferns had needed large amounts of water to reproduce, but plants with flowers could do this in drier conditions. Soon, flowering plants with brilliant-coloured blooms and powerful scents began to colonize every kind of **habitat** you can imagine. They grew on mountains, in deserts, and on cold, rocky plains – they even grew on each other. The world as it exists today was complete.

# 3

. . . . . . . . . . . . . . . . . . . . . . . . . . . .

# REVENGE OF THE KILLER VEGETABLES

The world is a very crowded place for plants. Most of the best habitats are already occupied, so some plants have had to look for somewhere different to put down their roots.

Bogs are promising places, because there is plenty of water, light and space and not much competition. But there is one thing missing which every plant must have – **nitrogen**.

Gardeners and farmers supply nitrogen fertilizer to their crops to encourage them to grow as fast and as large as possible. Rain quickly washes nitrogen away. Bogs are always found in wet places, so they contain very little of this vital element. Plants that live in bogs have been forced to look for new sources of nitrogen. To solve the problem, they have become **carnivorous**.

Insects, and all animals, are a main source of nitrogen. There is an endless supply of insects in the summer and flesh-eating plants have devised some cunning traps to catch them.

● **The jaws of death**
Years ago, poachers caught animals with horrible spring traps. These were like steel jaws containing long, spiky teeth that were held open by a metal plate. When a deer

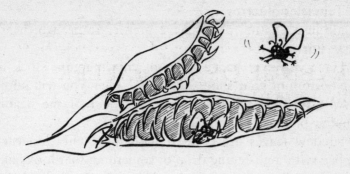

stepped on to the hidden plate, a powerful spring would snap the trap shut and that would be the end of the animal.

These gruesome traps were banned by law many years ago, but one plant uses something very similar to catch flies.

The leaves of the Venus fly-trap are fringed with long, spiky hairs and have a hinge down the middle. They tempt flies to land on them because they have the same dull-purple colour as rotten meat, something flies cannot resist.

Sometimes, when an insect lands on the surface of a leaf, nothing happens for several seconds, until it brushes against a trigger hair. Then – SNAP! – the leaf folds in half along the middle, like a book closing. The hairs along the edges link together like the bars of a cage – there is no escape!

Soon the walls of the prison become wet. Gooey juices, which are used to **digest** food, leak out of the leaf's surface and begin to dissolve the fly. The leaf then soaks up the digestive juices, which have become rich in fly-juice nitrogen. It slowly opens, and the dried, empty skin of the insect blows away in the wind.

### ● Tentacles of terror

Some insect-eating plants have prettier traps, which are just as dangerous.

Have you ever had a lump of chewing-gum stuck to the bottom of your shoe? You have? Then you will know how a fly feels when it lands on a leaf of the deadly sundew plant.

Sundew leaves are covered with long tentacles, each tipped with a glistening drop of something that looks like dew. But it's not dew, it's glue. When the insect lands, its feet and wings become stuck, just like your shoe when chewing-gum glues it to the pavement.

The more the insect struggles, the more tentacles it brushes against. Soon it becomes trapped. Tired, hungry and exhausted, it collapses. Then the tentacles begin to close over it and release the evil digestive juices. When they open again, a day or two later, there is almost nothing left. Just a few pieces of wing and a shrivelled leg or two.

### ● Death by drowning

Sundews and Venus fly-traps only catch small flies, but pitcher plants can capture larger prey. They have leaves that are rolled up in to long tubes that look like pitchers, with a pool of water at the bottom. Along the lip of the pitcher, and sometimes round the outside, there is a glistening trail of sweet nectar droplets. This is just too attractive for insects to ignore. Their sweet tooth lures them to their doom.

Once the insects reach the top of the pitcher and peer over the edge into the cavity inside, their feet become covered with loose scales of plant wax. It is as though the plant has fitted their feet with roller-skates, without them knowing. There can be no turning back, because sharp, pointed hairs bar the way. So the insects begin to slide down into the pitcher, faster and faster, until . . . well, I'll leave you to imagine the rest.

### • The bladders of doom

Perhaps the most amazing carnivorous plant of all is the bladderwort, which lives in bogs. Above the surface, this plant produces spikes of pretty yellow flowers. Under the water there are feathery leaves which are covered in little pots, or bladders, with hinged lids.

When the lid of the bladderwort bladder is closed, it pumps out water. When a small animal, such as a water-flea, swims past and accidentally brushes against a delicate trigger hair, the lid flies open. Water rushes in, carrying the water-flea with it, then the bladderwort lid slams shut. One second the water-flea is outside the bladder, the next it is trapped inside. It all happens in the blink of an eye. And I think that you can probably guess the rest of the gory details.

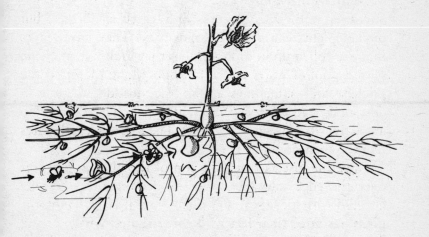

### • Hitch-hikers, thieves and stranglers

In dense forests there are hundreds of different types of plants, packed together in a small space. In order to survive in this crowded **environment**, some plants have had to use special tricks to get their share of the sunlight.

In forests where the leaves fall in winter, the tiny mosses on the ground make most of their growth in spring, before the canopy of leaves closes over their heads again.

Other plants have developed different methods. Polypody fern spores **germinate** in the dead leaves that collect in crevices in trees. Then they grow out along branches, among the leaves of the tree.

Climbers like ivy and honeysuckle grow in a similar way. They scramble up tree trunks towards the light.

Mistletoe has gone one step further. It has lost its roots altogether and joins up with the branches of the tree, stealing its host's supply of water and **nutrients**.

In tropical forests there are many plants that hitch a ride on trees. Urn plants grow on branches and have their leaves arranged in funnel-shaped whorls, which catch rainwater. All sorts of animals live in these plant paddling-pools – flies, mosquitoes and even frogs.

If you watch *Tarzan* films you will know all about lianas which have thick climbing stems that twine around branches and dangle to the ground.

But the most sinister characters in this scramble for light are the tropical strangling figs. Their seeds are often dropped by birds into the crevices of the branches of their hapless host. First they lower roots down to the ground and anchor themselves, then they send out shoots. As the strangler grows, its roots quickly thicken and begin to squeeze the trunk of its host until they slowly choke it to death. Eventually only the cylindrical trunk of the strangler fig is left. The host trunk inside rots away.

**FASTFACT:**
Its more than likely that you have a strangler in your home, because the weeping fig (*Ficus benjamina*), which is often sold as a houseplant, grows in exactly this way in its native jungles.

# 4

## FLOWERS FIGHT BACK

One way or another, plants are the food source for almost every animal on earth. They lie at the bottom of what biologists call food-chains, in which an animal eats a plant, then another animal eats the first animal, and so on. One example of a short food-chain is where cows eat grass and then we eat cows. Plants are constantly being eaten by hungry animals, but sometimes they fight back. Many have developed defence systems, which include:

* thorns and prickles to deter grazing animals. Plants like brambles, cacti, roses, holly and gorse use these.

* nasty-tasting chemicals and poisons in leaves. Many animals avoid rhubarb leaves, which contain poisonous oxalic acid crystals, for example.

* stinging hairs, which are found on nettles.

* sticky stems, which stop insects crawling upwards to eat the leaves.

* leaves that surround the stem like a cup and collect pools of rainwater. Teasels have leaves like this and insects that try to crawl past their water-traps drown.

● **The whistling thorn's private army**

Some plants have found a clever way to fight off hungry caterpillars. They have recruited their own private army of ants to protect them.

On the dry and dusty plains of Africa there are umbrella-shaped trees called Acacias. Some of these are known as whistling thorns because their thorns are swollen into hollow chambers, with small entrance holes. When the wind blows across the entrance holes it sounds like flutes playing in the branches.

You can show how this works by blowing across the top of a small, narrow-necked bottle and listening. Whistling thorns sound just the same on a windy day.

The hollow chambers of whistling thorns make excellent homes for ants. In exchange for these nests the ants protect the tree from caterpillars and other leaf-eating insects. They act as the trees' private army!

● **Desert dwellers**

Cacti and succulents have adapted to the burning heat

and chilly nights of the world's deserts. Their survival depends on special features that allow them to use water very economically:

* they have a thick waxy covering to keep water in;

* they have lost their leaves and replaced them with spines. This prevents water loss and keeps hungry animals at bay;

* they close the breathing pores in their surface in the day and open them at night. They have a special chemical system for absorbing vital carbon dioxide after dark;

* they have good root systems, that can reach deep water or, more often, spread just below the surface to absorb rare rainfall as soon as it lands;

* they have succulent stems to store water. Some desert plants also have underground **tubers** for water storage.

### ● Living stones
Food is in short supply in the desert, where there are many hungry animals. Instead of protecting itself with spines, the living stone (*Lithops*), from South Africa, is camouflaged to look like a stone. It is almost invisible until it flowers.

### ● Windows on the world
*Fenestraria* is a strange succulent with no spines. For protection from animals and the burning heat it lives buried in the sand, with just the tips of the leaves showing. These are transparent and act as windows, letting light through to the buried plant.

## FASTFACTS:

The saguaro, which often appears in cowboy films, is the largest cactus. It grows in Arizona and Mexico, lives for 150 years and reaches a height of over 18 metres.

The prickly pear cactus produces edible fruits. You can buy these in some large supermarkets. They taste very good, but you have to wear gloves when you peel them.

Besides cacti, there are also fast-growing annual plants in deserts. After a shower of rain their seeds germinate and the plants grow, flower and set seed in the space of a few weeks. Following rain the whole desert blooms for a short period.

# FLAMBOYANT FLOWERS

- **'An abominable mystery.'**
These were the words Charles Darwin used when he tried to explain when and where flowers first evolved. Unlike their more primitive relatives they left very few fossils. Fragile flowers rot quickly when they fall from plants and decay before they can be fossilized, so we will probably never know when the first flower opened.

One certain fact is that plants with flowers are one of **evolution**'s most successful experiments. Since they first appeared, perhaps 135 million years ago, flowering plants have managed to colonize almost every type of habitat that will support life. Another certainty is that we depend on them more than any other type of plant. They provide food, shelter, fibres, fuel and a host of other things that make our civilization possible.

Flowering plants are made of five main modules – stems, leaves, roots, flowers and seeds – but every one of these can vary in a host of different ways, producing an enormous variety of plant types.

## DATAFILE: THE FLOWERING PLANT IDENTIKIT

**PLANT MODULE: STEM**

**FUNCTION:**

  1. **Support.**

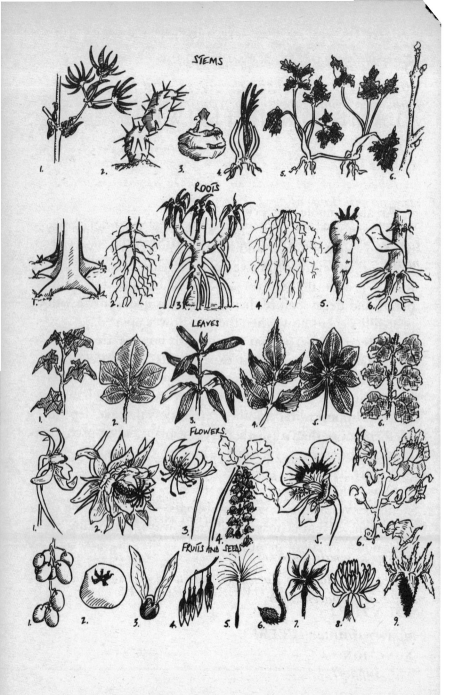

STEMS

1. 2. 3. 4. 5. 6.

ROOTS

1. 2. 3. 4. 5. 6.

LEAVES

1. 2. 3. 4. 5. 6.

FLOWERS

1. 2. 3. 4. 5. 6.

FRUITS AND SEEDS

1. 2. 3. 4. 5. 6. 7. 8. 9.

2. *Transportation of essential supplies.*

HOW IT WORKS: *Tough, reinforced structure packed with microscopic pipes which transport water, minerals and sugars up and down the plant into leaves, roots and flowers.*

APPEARANCE: *Variable. Can be long, short, thin, fat, branched, straight, woody or soft. Or almost anything else you can think of.*

TALLEST: *An Australian Eucalyptus regnans once grew to over 130 metres. The tallest tree still standing is a 110 metre high coast redwood.*

PLANT MODULE: ROOT

FUNCTION:

1. *Anchorage for the stem.*
2. *Absorption of water and mineral salts from soil. Some swollen roots, such as carrots, also contain food reserves.*

HOW IT WORKS:
*Grows through soil in search of water.*

APPEARANCE: *Variable. Storage roots are swollen. Most roots are long and branched. Tree roots may be woody.*

LONGEST: *Uncertain. Desert trees probably have roots which penetrate through hundreds of metres of sand and rock. Longest measured root is 120 metres long and belongs to a wild fig-tree.*

SMALLEST: *Floating duckweed has a root like a microscopic, transparent hair.*

PLANT MODULE: LEAF

FUNCTION:

1. *Energy capture.*

2. *Gas absorption and release.*
3. *Chemical synthesis.*
4. *Water transportation.*

HOW IT WORKS:

1. *Light energy is captured from the sun by the process of photosynthesis, using the* molecule *known as chlorophyll.*

2. *Carbon dioxide enters through the pores on the surface of the leaf called stomata. Gas is dissolved from the air into the wet surface of the cells.*

3. *The production of vital chemical compounds takes place in the cells. Water and carbon dioxide are converted into sugars. Waste oxygen is released into the atmosphere through the stomata.*

4. *Water evaporates from the surface of the leaf, cooling the plant and drawing water and dissolved food substances through the stem.*

APPEARANCE: *Many disguises. Can transform into stems and thorns. Normally flat green plates attached to stems.*

LARGEST: *Gunnera manicata from Brazil has leaves which are over 3 metres in diameter. Some Raffia palms and bamboos have leaves which are almost 20 metres long.*

LONGEST: *Lygodium fern has leaves that are 30 metres long.*

PLANT MODULE: FLOWER

FUNCTION:

1. *Attraction of insects and other animals for pollen transfer.*
2. *Reproduction of species.*

*HOW IT WORKS:*

1. *Bright colours and sweet nectar attract insects, which then carry the pollen between flowers.*

2. *Egg cells hidden in the base of the flower are fertilized by pollen and grow into seeds.*

*APPEARANCE: Masters of deception. Every colour, shape and size imaginable, and some that are not.*

*LARGEST: Rafflesia, from the jungles of Sumatra, is almost 1 metre across.*

*PLANT MODULE: SEED*

*FUNCTION: Survival capsule.*

*HOW IT WORKS: Miniature plant surrounded by a food store and enclosed in a tough, waterproof survival shield.*

*APPEARANCE: Masters of disguise. Some are covered in hooks, to catch in animal fur; some have parachutes; some are enclosed in succulent fruit and are eaten by animals (the tough seed-coat can survive passage through an animal's gut).*

*LARGEST: Lodoicia – the double coconut from Seychelles Islands. Takes six years to develop and weighs 18 kilograms.*

*SMALLEST: Orchid seed – invisible to naked eye. Some weigh less than one millionth of a gram.*

*LONGEST LIVED: Arctic lupin seeds have been germinated after being buried for at least 8,000 years in frozen mud.*

# 6

SWEET TEMPTATION –
HOW PLANTS PRODUCE SEEDS

Most plants spread by producing seeds. Seeds develop when **pollen** grains, which are the male parts of flowers produced on **stamens** land on **stigmas**, which are the female parts. Pollen begins to grow on the stigma, down towards the female egg cells and when it meets these a seed is produced.

So for seeds to be formed, plants have had to find a way to transfer pollen from stamens to stigmas. Sometimes the pollen must be carried between plants that are separated by great distances.

Many grasses, and trees such as hazel, have solved the problem in a simple way. They produce pollen in their florets or catkins, which is blown by the wind towards neighbouring plants. But this method means they must produce enormous amounts of pollen, to be sure that one pollen grain will safely arrive at its destination.

Other plants are more cunning. They trick insects into doing the job for them by offering a reward for carrying the pollen between plants. This is usually nectar, a sweet liquid which is the perfect source of energy for insects such as bees and butterflies.

If you look very closely at flowers, using a magnifying glass, you will see that there are often sticky drops of nectar near the base of the petals. Bees love it and so do we – because this is what bees use to make honey.

## DATAFILE: FLOWER VISITORS

VISITOR: *BEETLES*

FLOWER TYPES: *Often have fruity scent. Sometimes bowl-shaped. Usually have large numbers of stamens producing lots of pollen.*

EXAMPLE: *Magnolia trees.*

ADDITIONAL INFORMATION: *Beetles were probably the first plant* pollinators. *They eat parts of the flower and pollinate it by accident.*

VISITOR: *FLIES*

FLOWER TYPES: *Often traps. Often evil-smelling.*

EXAMPLE: *The voodoo lily from India, which has a terrible smell and has the same colour as rotting meat. It lures flies into a prison chamber, where they are trapped until they pollinate the flowers.*

ADDITIONAL INFORMATION: *Most of the spectacular fly pollinated flowers come from tropical countries. Flies receive no reward for pollinating flowers.*

VISITOR: *BEES.*

FLOWER TYPES: *Brightly coloured. Produce lots of nectar, often hidden in a tubular part of the flower, so only bees, with long tongues, can reach it. Occassionally have landing-platform for bee. Sometimes scented.*

EXAMPLE: *Broad-bean flower.*

ADDITIONAL INFORMATION: *Bees rely on nectar for an energy source and collect pollen to feed their young.*

VISITOR: *BUTTERFLIES*

FLOWER TYPES: *Pale colours. Nectar in long tubes that butterfly can reach with its long, coiled tongue. Often scented.*

EXAMPLE: *Fragrant orchids.*

VISITOR: *MOTHS*

FLOWER TYPES: *Pale colours. Have a strong scent at night and very long nectar tubes.*

EXAMPLE: *Honeysuckle.*

ADDITIONAL INFORMATION: *Angraecum sesquipedale, an orchid from Madagascar, has nectar hidden in a flower tube which is 45 centimetres long. There is only one moth with a 45 centimetre tongue that can reach it.*

VISITOR: *BIRDS*

FLOWER TYPES: *Almost always red. Lots of pollen and nectar. Some have a perch for the bird.*

EXAMPLES: *Fuchsia from South America is pollinated by humming-birds. It is often grown in gardens in Europe, where there are no humming-birds to pollinate it.*

VISITOR: *BATS*

FLOWER TYPES: *Large and strong, to resist damage from bat claws. Masses of nectar and pollen. Some smell like sour milk or goats!*

EXAMPLES: *The cup-and-saucer flower (Cobaea scadens) is visited by bats in Mexico. It is grown in gardens in many parts of the world.*

ADDITIONAL INFORMATION: *Bat pollination is very common in tropical rain forest trees.*

# 7

## PONGY PLANTS

Some plants trick insects into visiting them without giving a reward at all. The masters of this kind of deception include the world's pongiest plants, which smell like dead animals and attract flies from far and wide.

### • The stinking starfish flower
One plant which uses this trick is the starfish flower, or Stapelia, from Africa. Stapelias look just like brown and

yellow starfish sitting in the sand. To find out how they work all you need to do is bring your nose close to their petals. There are no polite words to describe how awful they smell, but I am sure you can think of something!

Flies think the starfish flowers are pieces of rotten meat, which would make the perfect place to raise a family. They lay their eggs on the surface, accidentally pollinating the flower at the same time. But when the maggots hatch out there is no rotten meat for them to feed on, so they die.

### • Beccari's stink bomb

The most spectacular pongy plant of them all is the titan, also known by the tongue-twisting name of *Amorphophallus titanum*. This was discovered by an Italian explorer called Odoardo Beccari, in the jungles of Sumatra, in 1878.

Odoardo could smell the plant long before he could see it. It filled the jungle with a stench which he said was like a combination of burned sugar and rotting fish. The Titan attracted swarms of flies, all tricked into believing that they would get a free, disgusting meal.

Beccari marked the spot where the giant plant stood and when the flower died down, he came back and dug up the massive tuber that the plant had sprouted from. It was so large it took two of his assistants to carry it out of the jungle, slung from a pole which they carried on their shoulders!

When the plant arrived in Europe it was grown in a greenhouse in Kew Gardens, where people waited patiently for it to flower. When its two metre high bloom finally appeared they were not disappointed. The smell was so bad that no one would go into the greenhouse. They all peered through the glass at it. After a few short hours the flower wilted and died, but everyone who was there remembered its awful smell until their dying day!

● **A plant that takes prisoners**

In Britain and Europe cuckoo-pint (*Arum maculatum*) is a miniature version of the titan and flowers every spring. It is a peculiar plant, with a hooded flower that contains a club-shaped purple structure called a spadix. When the flower opens the spadix begins to heat up, giving off an evil smell that attracts small flies and midges.

When they reach the plant they walk towards the base of the flower into a swollen chamber which is protected by downward-pointing hairs. Once inside, the hairs stop the flies or midges from escaping until they have pollin-ated the tiny flowers. When this has happened the hairs wilt and the plant lets its prisoners escape.

**FASTFACT:**
**Cuckoo-pint grows from underground tubers that contain starch. This was used to stiffen the enormous white ruffs that Elizabethan courtiers wore around their necks.**

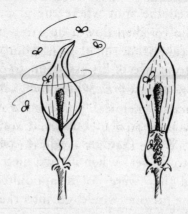

## • The vegetable bumble-bee

Evil smells are just one of many ways in which plants trick insects into working for them. Some orchids are even more cunning.

Bee orchids look just like bees. Their centres look like a furry body, with two wings, a head and antennae sprouting from it. To a male bee, a bee orchid flower looks just like a female bee. In fact, it even smells like a female bee!

The females of some insects, such as moths and bees, produce secret chemicals called **pheromones**, which our noses cannot detect but which attract male insects from miles around. Somehow, bee orchids have learned to make this attractive chemical. Male bees are unable to resist it, so they land on the bee orchid and try to mate with the flower. While they are doing this they accidentally pollinate it.

# 8

. . . . . . . . . . . . . . . . . . . . . . . .

# ROCKET-PROPELLED CUCUMBERS AND OTHER WAYS OF SCATTERING SEEDS

Once plants have successfully produced seeds, they must scatter them efficiently. If the seeds just dropped to the ground, there would soon be a forest of seedlings. They would choke each other to death in their struggle for light and water.

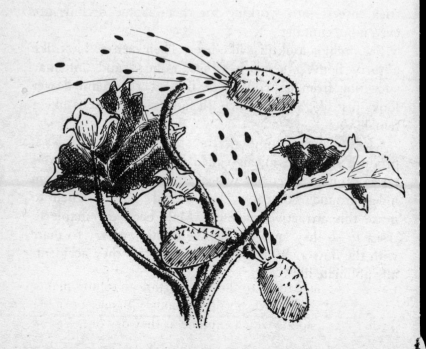

The most spectacular seed dispersal mechanism belongs to the squirting cucumber, which grows in the countries around the shores of the Mediterranean. If you accidentally walked into a patch of this plant, which grows about 30 centimetres high, you would think you were being attacked by a hidden tribe of tiny people armed with pea-shooters and water-pistols.

The flowers of the plant develop into swollen cucumbers, each about 5 centimetres long, which swell until they almost explode. When the stem of the cucumber cannot stand the pressure any longer it suddenly lets go. All the juices and seeds inside the cucumber squirt out through the hole left by the stem. This is exactly the same principle that is used in rocket-engines for space vehicles.

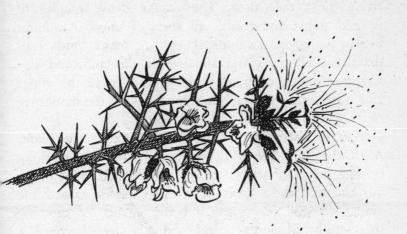

● **Exploding pods**

You do not have to go to the Mediterranean to find plants with spectacular seed dispersal methods. Gorse is a prickly shrub that has pods which explode as they dry out.

As the pod develops some parts of it grow faster than others. Some bits become woody, while others keep swelling, so parts of the pod are pushed and pulled in different directions. When the pod is ripe it only needs the gentlest touch to make it fly apart and scatter its seeds. If you sit beside a gorse bush on a hot, sunny day in late summer you can hear a constant series of explosions and the patter of seeds as they fall to the ground.

### ● Mangroves on the move

Most plants scatter their seeds and hope for the best. Some seeds might be eaten by animals, or buried, or just dry up in the sun. But one plant, the mangrove, takes no chances. It deliberately plants its seeds.

Mangroves grow in swamps on the edge of tropical rivers, near the coast. They make dense jungles of twisted stems and roots. All sorts of unusual animals live in mangrove swamps. There are snakes and crabs that have left the water and live on the land, and also strange fish, called mud skippers, that leave the water and walk over the wet, slimy mud among the mangrove roots.

Mangrove seeds germinate while still fixed to the plant. A slender root grows downwards. When this is long enough the plant lets go of the seed, which plops down into the mud like a spear. With its root safely buried, the mangrove seed has a much better chance of growing successfully. Mangrove swamps slowly creep forward, a few metres every year, as each generation of seeds is produced.

### ● Seeds in your socks

You do not need to go to exotic places to discover the cunning tricks that plants use to spread their seeds around. All you need to do is take a walk in the country-side in summer or early autumn.

If you look at your socks when you get home you will probably find the seeds of goose-grass (some people call this plant 'sticky jack'). Look at these with a magnifying glass and you will see they are covered with tiny hooks, which were designed to become trapped in the fur of animals such as rabbits and mice, but socks are just as good!

### ● Plant parachutists
Lots of plants such as dandelions and thistles, have seeds that are fitted with tiny parachutes, which can carry the seeds for miles on the breeze.

### ● Whirling woodlands
The seeds of trees such as sycamore and maple have wings, which make them spin like a helicopter as they fall to earth. This enables the seeds to be carried away on the wind.

## • Flying fruit

For long-distance travel some plants have developed another trick. The outside of the seed has a succulent, tasty covering that birds and animals like to eat. When a bird such as a missel-thrush eats a holly berry, it digests the soft, fleshy fruit, but the hard, woody shell of the seed is protected from the acidic digestive juices of the bird's stomach. Eventually the seed is passed out of the bird, in a bird-dropping, but by the time this happens the bird may have flown many miles.

Fruits like this, with edible coverings that tempt birds and animals to eat them, are very common, especially in tropical countries. Tomatoes, grapes, bananas, cherries and strawberries are all designed to attract animals in this way. Elder bushes, which often spring up in guttering on the edge of a roof, have grown from seeds that have passed through the digestive system of a bird.

FASTFACT:
When the volcano on the island of Krakatoa exploded in 1883 the island was destroyed. Continued small eruptions produced a new island, called Son of Krakatoa, which first appeared above the waves in 1928. To begin with there were no signs of life, but soon plants began to appear on the volcanic larva. They had been carried there inside visiting birds.

# 9

. . . . . . . . . . . . . . . . . . . . . . . . . . . . . .

# THE NAME GAME

The first cavemen were hunter-gatherers, trapping animals and searching out fruits and seeds for food. They learned which animals were easy to trap and which plants were not poisonous by trial and error. They made many painful, and sometimes fatal, mistakes. But those who survived began naming plants and animals and parents used these names to pass on their precious knowledge to their sons and daughters. But, they soon ran into a serious problem. Individual tribes often gave different names to the same plant. This made it very difficult for them to exchange useful information.

This problem still exists today. There are at least 112 names for the plant that some people call cuckoo-pint, others call wild arum, and which is also known as lords and ladies.

Different local or national names for the same plant can be very confusing, so biologists give each plant and animal a single Latin name. The scientific, Latin name for cuckoo-pint (or whatever *you* like to call it) is *Arum maculatum*.

Every scientist in the world understands what you mean when you call a potato by its Latin name, *Solanum tuberosum*. Unfortunately, not many other people do! If you go into a fish and chip shop and ask for a bag of fried *Solanum tuberosum*, you will probably get some funny looks!

## • Lobivia from Bolivia

How do plants get their names? Sometimes the name actually describes the plant. If you see *tuberosum* in the name, it means the plant produces tubers. If you see the word *purpureum* in the name, it means that the plant is purple.

With so many plants to catalogue, botanists sometimes run out of ideas for names. One of the strangest names belongs to a Bolivian cactus. Botanists argued about what to call it, until someone hit on a brilliant idea. Why not rearrange the letters of the word Bolivia, to make a new word that they could use for the plant? So eventually they swopped the b and the l and decided to call it *lobivia*. *Lobivia* from Bolivia. At least it is one of the easier Latin names to remember!

Words like this, which are made by rearranging the letters of other words, are called anagrams. Another plant with an anagram name is *Jacaima*, which comes from Jamaica. Here are a few anagrams from the names of some common plants. See if you can work out what their real, common names are.

PITUL FODDILAF YASID BAGECAB NEDILONDA

## • The rules of the game

Latin names always come in two parts. The first is called the genus and always starts with a capital letter. The second part is the specific name and always begins with a small letter.

| _Arum_ | _maculatum_ = | cuckoo-pint | (or 112 other names!) |
|---|---|---|---|
| (Genus) | (species) | (Common name) | |

Incidentally, _maculatum_ means 'spotty' – cuckoo-pint often has black spots on its leaves. This is the only species in the genus _Arum_ in Britain, but fourteen more species grow in Europe.

● **The referee**
The man who invented the two-part naming system we use today was a Swede, called Linnaeus, who lived from 1707 to 1778. Before he came along with his simple rules, people often wrote long descriptions of each plant in Latin. He shortened these to just two words.

FASTFACTS:
* Sometimes plants are named after ancient gods, like _Heracleum_ (hogweed), which is named after Hercules.
* Many plants are named after people. If you are a scientist one of the greatest honours is to have a plant or animal named after you. _Berberis darwinii_ is the name of a beautiful, orange-flowered shrub that was discovered by Charles Darwin in South America.
* The shortest Latin name is _Aa_, and belongs to a tropical American orchid.
* No one is too sure what the longest name is but there are plenty that are difficult to pronounce. Try saying _Rhododendron schlippenbachii_, _Paeonia mlokosewitschii_ and _Zantedeschia aethiopica_ as fast as you can and you will see what I mean!

# 10

# IS IT A PLANT?
# IS IT AN ANIMAL?
# NO, IT'S A FUNGUS!

Fungi have always been a bit of a problem. Scientists like to classify living things into neat categories but the mushrooms and toadstools don't really seem to fit anywhere.

In many ways they are like plants, but without any green pigment. This means that they cannot make their own food from carbon dioxide and water, like normal plants do. Instead they send microscopic, wandering threads called **hyphae** through living and dead things. As the hyphae creep forward they release chemicals called **enzymes**, that dissolve away their surroundings and leave a pool of nutrients that the fungal threads can absorb. This is why food that is infected with fungi feels squashy – it is being dissolved by these destructive secretions.

But in other ways some fungi are like animals. The

slime moulds, which often look like blobs of coloured custard, can move. They begin life as millions of microscopic cells that crawl over surfaces feeding on bacteria. Then they come together to create a kind of creeping custard that eventually dries out and turns into millions of powdery **spores**.

Nowadays, most scientists believe that fungi are neither plants or animals but are – well – just fungi. There is nothing else quite like them. But the one thing everyone agrees on is that they are extraordinarily important. We depend on them for food, drink, medicine and the health of the environment. At the same time we need to fight endlessly to keep the rogue fungi that attack us and our crops, at bay.

### ● Living waste disposal units

If there were no fungi, we would have been buried in dead plants a long time ago. In autumn, when the leaves fall from the trees, it is mainly the activity of fungi that breaks them down into humus in the soil. The leaves on the woodland floor in autumn are like a giant compost heap, riddled with creeping fungal hyphae that are quietly working away, dissolving dead leaves and enriching the soil.

### Making a spore print

Buy a large, flat mushroom from the supermarket. Try to find one where the gills underneath are undamaged.

Cut the cap from the stalk and place it, gill-side downwards, on a sheet of white paper and leave it overnight in a room where there are no draughts. When you lift the cap in the morning you will find a perfect, radiating pattern of brown spores on the paper. If you spray this with artists' varnish when it is dry this will prevent the pattern smudging.

CUT OFF THE STALK.

PLACE CAP ON PAPER –
GILL-SIDE DOWN.

REMOVE CAP – SPORE PATTERN
PRINTED ON PAPER.

Every so often, when the fungal hyphae are well-fed, a miraculous change happens. By a process that no one really understands, the hyphae come together and form a small egg-shaped structure, that pushes up to the surface of the soil, where it opens out into the familiar shape of a mushroom or toadstool.

On the underside of a mushroom there are flat plates called gills, which radiate out from the central stalk like spokes of a bicycle wheel. On the surface of these gills microscopic, round cells called spores are formed, they rain down in their millions and are carried away by the wind. There are billions of fungal spores in the air. They are everywhere. Every lungful of air that you breath contains some.

When the spores land on a suitable food supply the whole process begins again as they germinate and send out creeping hyphae, which once more steadily dissolve their way through their surroundings.

**FASTFACT:**
**Giant puffball fungi can grow to over 2 metres in diameter.**

● **Fungal medicine**
Not all fungi produce mushrooms. Some just grow as expanding colonies of hyphae that produce powdery spores on their surfaces. Many of the destructive moulds, like the green one that grows on rotting oranges, form colonies like this.

It was a mould that led to one of the greatest breakthroughs in medical history. One day in 1928 a scientist called Alexander Fleming was clearing up his laboratory, where he had been growing various harmful bacterium on the surface of nutrient jelly. As he turned to wash up a pile of containers he noticed one with a mysterious greenish-blue mould that seemed to have killed all the bacteria around it. The green mould was called *Penicillium* and when its anti-bacterial secretion was extracted and purified it was named penicillin.

Penicillin is what is known as an **antibiotic** and it has saved countless thousands of lives. It is very effective in killing bacteria that attack humans. If you have ever had a really bad sore throat or ear-ache the doctor may have prescribed an antibiotic for you. It was Fleming's mystery fungus that took away your pain.

### ● Wine . . .

No one really knows how people learned to make wine, but it might have happened by accident. If you look closely at the surface of a red grape or a plum you can seen a powdery material, which often gives the fruit a blue sheen. This is easy to rub off and is made up of the cells of a fungus called yeast.

Yeast feeds by breaking down sugary substances that leak through the skin of fruits. As it grows it makes alcohol as one of its waste products. If the fruit is crushed and left in water the alcohol builds up, until it becomes concentrated enough to kill the yeast. Then the whole process, known as **fermentation**, comes to a halt.

Perhaps people first encountered the pleasant effects of wine when they drank water that fruit had fermented in and became slightly drunk. Wine certainly became popular early in history. Today, brewing is a multi-million pound industry, which depends for its success on yeast, the tiny fungus on the surface of fruits.

● **. . . and bread**

These same yeast cells produce another waste product when they ferment sugar. This is the gas carbon dioxide.

If you eat bread in many Middle Eastern countries you will find that it is flat and not spongy like the bread we eat in Europe and North America. We add yeast to our dough and by allowing bread to stand for a short time before we cook it, we allow the fungus to begin fermenting the starch in the flour, producing bubbles of carbon dioxide gas, which make the dough rise.

When the bread is baked the dough hardens, trapping the air bubbles and giving bread a light, spongy consistency.

● **Fungal killers**

Not all fungal waste products are as welcome as the alcohol and carbon dioxide produced by yeast. Some are deadly poisons. Every year people die after eating toadstools which they thought were edible.

The deadliest of these is the death cap. This can be recognized by its greenish cap, a frill around the stem and a bulbous base. It causes many deaths from fungal poisoning. The terrible thing about eating death caps is that the victims feel no ill effects for a day or two, and when they do appear it is usually too late to save them. Victims suffer a slow and agonizing death. So you should only eat wild toadstools if you are certain that they are edible. Mistaken identification can be fatal.

FASTFACTS:
FUNGAL FOES
Fungi are notorious spoilers. They attack our homes, our food, and even us.

\* Dry rot creeps under the floor-boards and through the

dark cavities of our homes, dissolving away the strong fibres of wood until they crumble to dust.

* Moulds attack stored products like food, leather and books. In many tropical countries moulds spoil much of the food that is harvested, making it unfit to eat and leading to famine. Moulds that attack peanuts, for example, produce aflotoxin, one of the deadliest fungal poisons.

* Fungi grow in the most surprising places, like fuel tanks. Snow moulds can grow at low temperatures, destroying lawns under a layer of snow.

* Rust fungi attack crops, such as wheat and maize. Sometimes epidemics of these parasites can wipe out millions of acres of crops.

* Some fungi even attack us, causing skin problems like athlete's foot or lung infections.

Fungi are everywhere, in uncountable numbers. There are many more species that scientists have yet to discover. Out task is to find ways of preventing the damaging fungi from doing their destructive work and at the same time exploiting the useful products that fungi produce.

**FASTFACT:**

One of the latest developments is the production of meat substitutes made from fungi that are grown in huge containers of nutrients. This fungal 'meat' is known as mycoprotein. It is an ideal source of protein for vegetarians, who do not want to eat meat.

# 11

FEEDING THE WORLD

Mankind uses about 1,500 plant species as food but grasses are the most important of all the edible plants. Their seeds contain **starch**, **protein**, fats and vitamins – all essential components of a healthy diet.

Humans have been cultivating different grasses for their seeds for at least 10,000 years, since the beginning of civilization. Generations of farmers and scientists have selected varieties with larger and more nutritious grains, so that modern crops produce the high yields which are needed to feed the world's rapidly growing population.

## FASTFACTS:
## GRASS SEEDS THAT FEED THE WORLD

* Rice is the main source of energy for half of the world's population and is the staple food for the peoples of Asia. The brown outer coat of rice grains is usually milled off, so that the rice cooks faster. This also removes much of the valuable protein, so people whose diet mainly consists of rice must eat other food, such as peas and beans, to ensure that they get enough protein.
* Wheat is the most important cereal in Europe. Wild wheat still grows in parts of the Middle East. Wheat is

used to make bread and for the production of foods like biscuits and breakfast cereals. It is also fed to farm animals.

* Barley is an important European and Middle Eastern cereal, which is often fed to farm animals. It is also used in the brewing industry.

* Oats are mainly grown for animal feed but are also made into breakfast cereals and used to make porridge.

* Maize, which is called corn in the United States, is one of the world's most important cereals. It has been grown for at least 7,000 years in tropical America. The grains are carried on large cobs, which are eaten as a vegetable (corn-on-the-cob). In many parts of the world maize is also grown to feed farm animals.

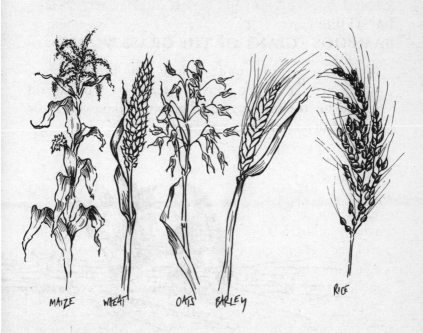

MAIZE   WHEAT   OATS   BARLEY   RICE

The leaves of the grass family grow in a way that makes them perfect for grazing animals such as cows. The long, narrow leaves grow from the base, so the tip of the leaf is the oldest part. When an animal eats the top of the leaf it will continue to grow from the base, so that the animal can come back a few days later and eat it again. In this way pastures can be grazed almost continuously by herds of animals, provided that the animals are removed at regular intervals, to allow the leaves to regrow.

This kind of growth also means that grass is the ideal surface for lawns and outdoor sports pitches that are used for games like tennis and football. The grass can be mown short without killing it, because the mower blades do not reach the part of the leaf that grows, which is close to the soil surface.

## FACTFILE:
## BAMBOOS – GIANT OF THE GRASS WORLD

* Most grasses grow quite quickly but the bamboos, which are the largest grasses of all, hold the world record for the fastest rate of growth. Some will grow more than 90 centimetres per day.

* Some bamboos are so large it is hard to believe that they are grass just like your lawn! The largest will reach a height of over 30 metres in a few months. In tropical countries their woody stems are often used to build houses.

* Bamboos are often long-lived. They die in a most unusual way. All the individuals of a particular species suddenly flower at once, wherever they happen to be growing. This occurs at regular intervals, of thirty-three to sixty-six years. Once the plants have flowered they die and disappear from the scene, until new plants grow from seed. This mass suicide of the bamboo plants can be disastrous for animals such as the giant panda, because bamboo-shoots are its main food.

## • Spicy tales

For thousands of years plants have been used to add flavour to food. In Europe many herbs are used, such as a sprig of mint added to boiled potatoes, rosemary sprinkled on fatty food like lamb or thyme and marjoram added to pizza.

In India carefully blended herbs and spices, such as coriander and cumin, are used to make the curry powders

that give Indian food its hot and spicy taste. In Mexico chillis are used to make hot dishes, like chilli-con-carne.

There is another reason for adding spices to food, besides the flavour that they contribute. Modern research has shown that the scented oils in plants like summer savory can kill bacteria, so food can be stored a little longer.

Herbs and spices have always been highly valued. Even today saffron, which is made from the stigmas of crocus flowers, fetches a very high price. In the past herbs and spices were almost as valuable as gold. Countries sent explorers to the far corners of the world to find new ones, and fought battles for control of the sources of supply. One of the prizes which Christopher Columbus brought back to Spain from America were seeds of the red pepper.

### ● The nutmeg wars

Five different nations struggled for control of the highly prized seed of the nutmeg tree. Until the Portuguese

explorer Vasco da Gama discovered the Spice Islands in 1512, nutmegs were only available from Arab traders. Once he had found the nutmeg trees in the Far East their location was kept secret until the Dutch snatched the islands from the Portuguese. The Dutch merchants burned all the trees, except those on the island of Amboina. This meant that they could control world trade in nutmegs and keep the price high, but eventually the French and then the British managed to smuggle seeds out and start their own plantations.

- **Spice spies**

Cloves are the dried flower buds of a tropical tree. They were an expensive luxury in the ancient world and the Arabs controlled trade until European explorers discovered clove trees in the Spice Islands. There the Dutch guarded them jealously and destroyed trees to keep cloves in short supply and drive up prices. However, the French mounted a special secret expedition to smuggle clove seeds out to the island of Ceram, where they flourished, and undermined the Dutch traders' profitable business. Meanwhile the Sultan of Zanzibar managed to get his hands on clove trees too, planted them on his islands, and soon became a major producer. Today Zanzibar is the world's main supplier of cloves and clove oil.

# 12

. . . . . . . . . . . . . . . . . . . . . . . . . . .

# A PLANT FOR EVERY PURPOSE

How often do you have a bath? Once a month? I expect it is a bit more often than that, because if you did not you would soon begin to pong a bit.

These days having a bath is very easy because most houses have heating systems that provide plenty of hot water. But hundreds of years ago things were more difficult. Imagine taking a bath in freezing-cold water in a draughty castle in the middle of winter. Not a very pleasant prospect. So people did not wash very often. And, to be honest, by the time the bathing season came around in spring, they probably smelled like polecats. So to make life bearable rich people used a lot of scent.

## • Perfumes

Exotic scents have always been expensive and many of the most important ones come from plants. Two of the three precious gifts that the Three Wise Men gave to the infant Jesus Christ were incense and myrrh, which are both fragrant resins extracted from trees.

These sweet-smelling presents were as valuable as gold, because incense and myrrh trees only grew in Dhofar in Oman. The Sultan was extremely secretive about his valuable trees and in order to deter thieves he spread stories that they were guarded by winged serpents that hung from the branches. It was only in the nineteenth century that the priceless trees were discovered by foreigners and the secret was out.

Today, myrrh is still used in the most expensive French perfumes.

### • Vegetable air-fresheners

Hygiene was not something that people thought too much about back in the Middle Ages. They kept lots of animals in their houses and the floors were soon covered in rubbish and various other things that it's best not to even think about. And there were rats, thousands of them, spreading disease.

Rats carried the fleas that spread the Black Death, or Great Plague, which killed half the population of Europe between 1347 and 1354.

In order to combat the various nasty smells that tended to build up in their houses, people covered the floors with strewing herbs. These were plants that smelled pleasant when they dried, such as sweet flag (a kind of iris), meadowsweet (which has an antiseptic smell) and lady's bedstraw (which smells like newly mown hay). In fact, lady's bedstraw smells so nice that people used to stuff their mattresses with it, to help them sleep at night. King Henry VIII slept on a mattress stuffed with lady's bedstraw.

Other plants were used to get rid of insects. Herbs such as tansy were quite effective at this. People also used a fungus, the fly agaric toadstool, to trap flies. This is easily recognized by its red cap covered in white spots. They used to float pieces of the toadstool in a bowl of milk and the poison in the fungus would kill any flies that came to feed.

**FASTFACT:**
Do you remember this nursery rhyme?

> Ring-o-ring-o-roses, a pocket full of posies;
> Atishoo, atishoo, we all fall down!

Some people think that it might be about the Black Death. The first line is about the rings of red spots that the disease caused. When the Plague was at its height frightened people believed that if you carried a posy of flowers it would protect you from the disease. If it did not work you would 'all fall down' dead.

### • Colourful characters

Today most of our clothes are dyed bright colours by using chemicals that scientists have made in laboratories. Until the beginning of this century many dyes were produced from plants. By carefully selecting the right plant species most colours could be produced.

* Henna is a golden-brown dye that people still use to colour their hair. It is produced from a bush called Lawsonia, which grows in the Middle East.
* Woad is a blue dye, extracted from a plant in the cabbage family. The ancient Britons used it to colour their bodies. Together with indigo, a tropical plant, it was one of the few sources of blue colouring before modern chemical dyes were invented.
* Lichens produce delicate pastel shades of brown, green and yellow, which are still sometimes used for dyeing wool.
* Red dyes can be made from bloodroot, lady's bedstraw roots, madder and sorrel roots.
* Yellow and orange shades come from agrimony flowers, dyers greenweed, heather shoots and onion skins.
* Green dyes can be made from bracken, dog's mercury, nettle and privet.

● **The green medicine chest**
We have a lot to thank modern medicine for. In the Middle Ages, people who felt ill would visit their local apothecary, who specialized in herbal remedies. After they had described their symptoms he would open a massive book, called a herbal, which contained descriptions of plants that could be used as medicines.

Many of these plants really could cure peoples' illnesses but some were not very reliable. Apothecaries chose their plants according to what they called the Doctrine of Signatures. This meant that any plant that looked like a part of the body would cure its diseases. So a walnut, which looks a bit like a brain, was supposed to cure pains in the head. Liverworts were good for the liver, nipplewort was good for sore nipples and woundwort

## *Try a dye*

Ask an adult to boil some red cabbage leaves and save the juice for you. When it is **cold** pour a small amount into two glasses. Add vinegar to one and ask an adult to add a few crystals of washing soda to the other. Watch how the liquids change colour. Plants are full of coloured dyes like this.

BOIL RED CABBAGE TO PRODUCE BLUE JUICE.

PORE THE BLUE JUICE INTO TWO JARS.

ADD VINEGAR TO ONE — IT GOES BRIGHT PINK.
ADD WASHING SODA TO THE OTHER — IT WILL GO BRIGHT GREEN.

healed wounds. You can be sure that any plant with the word 'wort' in its name was used by apothecaries.

If you had toothache they would prescribe toothwort. This is a strange, white **parasite** which grows on the roots of hazel bushes. Its flowers look like a row of dirty teeth, so according to the Doctrine of Signatures it was supposed to cure toothache.

It was useless. Even if it had worked, there would not have been much point in going to your local apothecary with toothache in summer because toothwort flowers in the spring and then disappears. You would have had to wait for almost a year before you could collect your prescription.

### ● Got a headache?

Some of the herbal remedies really did work. If you had a headache, your apothecary would tell you to boil willow bark and drink the potion. Scientists now know that willow bark, and parts of several other plants, contain natural aspirin and can cure headaches. About ninety years ago scientists learned how to make aspirin in the laboratory, so these days, if you do not feel well, you can

take an aspirin tablet. Chewing willow twigs is NOT recommended.

## • Leafy lifesavers

There are hundreds of plants which contain useful medicines and many more that remain undiscovered. This is one of the reasons why it is so important to protect plants from extinction – there might be a plant in the jungle that could save your life one day.

A good example of this is the rosy periwinkle from Madagascar. Scientists have discovered it contains a drug which can save the lives of children who have certain types of cancer.

The bark of the Pacific yew tree produces a valuable drug called taxol, which is being used to fight cancer.

## FASTFACTS:

Moreton Bay chestnut, a plant that Captain Cook discovered on his voyages to Australia in 1770, is being used in the battle to treat the AIDS virus.

## • The alchemists' dream

Alchemists were medieval scientists who dreamed of finding the secret plants that would turn iron and lead into precious metals, like gold and silver. They were convinced that they could become fantastically rich by unlocking the secret of this magic process, which they called transmutation.

If you had been out walking early on a summer's morning about 500 years ago, you might have come across an alchemist in a meadow, bending low in search of magic herbs and mumbling strange words to himself.

He would have been looking for a plant called *Alchemilla*, which means 'the little alchemist.' The glistening

droplets of dew that clung to the edges of the leaf were a vital part of the transmutation recipe.

He would also have been looking for moonwort, an unusual fern that was used in potions aiming to turn lead into silver. Of course it would only work if it was collected while the moon was still in the sky! And, needless to say, none of these potions were any good. If they had worked I would not be telling you about them. I would be busy collecting *Alchemilla* and moonwort, so that I could become a millionaire!

• **Tulipomania**
It was a visit by the Austrian ambassador to the Emperor Suleiman the Magnificent in 1554 that started a craze which swept Europe, making fortunes for some men and reducing others to paupers.

The ambassador spied a tulip growing in a garden near Suleiman's palace in Constantinople (now called Istanbul). After much bargaining he bought a few bulbs, for an exorbitant amount.

He hurried back to Vienna with his prize and when the rich, fashionable Europeans saw the spectacular flowers they just had to have some in their gardens. The bulbs, which were in short supply to begin with, changed hands at ever-increasing prices.

Soon new varieties were produced, in exotic colours. In Holland tulipomania set in and the city of Haarlem became a centre for the tulip trade. The best bulbs were bought and sold for hundreds or even thousands of guilders. One man paid the record price of 13,000 guilders for a single bulb of a variety called *semper augustus*, another paid 4,600 guilders and swapped two grey horses and a fine carriage for one. These were enormous sums of money in the seventeenth century.

But, like skateboards, teenage mutant hero turtles and all other crazes, tulips soon went out of fashion. Tulipomania reached its height in 1634. In 1637 there came the Great Tulip Crash. Prices plummeted and merchants were ruined overnight.

But the legacy of tulipomania still remains. If you visit Haarlem in spring you will find fields full of millions of tulips, which are exported all over the world. Tulips are still a major industry.

**FASTFACT:**
**Today many plants are still extremely valuable. The price for an ounce of the seeds of some of the best varieties of primrose is over ten times more than an ounce of gold!**

# 13

. . . . . . . . . . . . . . . . . . . . . . . .

# TREES AND FORESTS

Each year tree growth begins when buds burst and produce new leafy shoots. As the season continues this growth becomes hard and woody. Then, the next year, while a new shoot forms, the previous year's shoots produce a ring of new cells which divide and harden to become a new layer of woody tissue within the old shoots.

In this way twigs grow longer and fatter until they become large branches. As branches and trunks grow thicker, the old outer cells die. They form tough, dead bark that protects the living cells inside. Growth of the stem often causes the bark to split into patterns.

When a tree is cut down, each year of growth can be seen as a ring of dead cells. Count the number of rings and you will soon find out how old a tree is. These rings of growth give wooden objects an attractive grain pattern. Some trees are famous for this. 'Fiddleback' maple, which has a swirling grain pattern, is used to make the backs of stringed instruments, such as violins. The bold, rippling grain of pine is good for making decorative furniture.

## ● Deciduous trees
Deciduous trees are the ones which drop all of their leaves every autumn and their branches remain bare

**Bark patterns**

*You can collect bark patterns by placing a large sheet of paper over a piece of bark and rubbing a large, flat wax crayon over the surface. The pattern will appear on the paper. Barks with a bold pattern, like sweet chestnut and oak, work best.*

through the cold winter months. They do this because the leaves would be damaged by frost. Leaves might also lose water when the ground is frozen and then no water would be available to the roots, so that the tree might suffer from drought.

Before deciduous trees shed their leaves they reabsorb all the green chlorophyll from the leaves, which is then broken down and transported back into the trunk. All that is left are a few brightly coloured pigments that the tree will not need and these produce the wonderful displays of autumn colour that we see in woodlands in the days before the leaves finally fall off.

● **Evergreen trees**

Evergreen trees also drop their leaves, but not all at once. The best-known evergreens are the conifers, like Christmas trees. Their needle-shaped leaves live for three or four years before they become too old to work properly and fall off the tree. So in a coniferous forest there is a constant rain of old needles falling to the ground, every month of the year.

Conifers are usually found in the higher, colder parts of the world. They can keep their leaves in winter because they have become adapted to the harsh conditions. Each leaf is covered with a thick layer of wax to prevent water loss and they also continue to carry out photosynthesis at low temperatures.

Most of the trees in tropical rain forests are also evergreens. They can keep their leaves because in the tropical regions there are no clear seasons and cold winters never occur.

● **Forests**

Forests have always been good habitats for humans. They provide a plentiful supply of food and for centuries people relied on them to provide fruits and seeds, and animals like deer and birds, that they could trap.

Wood burns easily, providing fuel that can be used for cooking and to provide heat. It is also a wonderful building material which is easy to cut, and is ideal for making houses and furniture.

When primitive people realized that wood floated they began to make boats and explore the land along the rivers and coast. Trees have been essential for our survival and the exploration of our surroundings.

● **A natural green blanket**

Most habitats develop into woodland if they are left

undisturbed. Tree seeds invade open land, either because they are dropped by passing birds or blown in on the wind. When they germinate they form scrub and then woodland. Before humans arrived most of Europe was covered with woodland, except during the Ice Ages.

When the first settlers landed in America they found vast tracts of forest extending to the horizon, although some woodland had already been cleared when the native Indians burned it. Often the forests were so dense that the only way to explore inland was by boat, along rivers.

Today the world's great forests are disappearing fast, as people clear the land for agriculture and building. The last remaining examples of really large areas of forestation are some of the old coniferous forests in both northern Siberia and America, and the tropical rain forests of the Amazon. Even these are being cut down or burned.

### • The lungs of the world

Forests play a major role in absorbing carbon dioxide from the atmosphere and storing it in their trunks. One of the reasons why we are threatened by **global-warming** is that trees can no longer remove enough carbon dioxide from the air to prevent the **greenhouse effect** from becoming more powerful.

The destruction of tropical rain forests is a disaster for another reason. They are home to many of the world's most unusual and beautiful animals and plants. Tropical orchids, birds of paradise, monkeys, bats, and big cats like jaguars live there. Useful plants that provide foods and medicine are just a few of the natural treasures that are disappearing.

Rain forests, where the air is always warm and wet, are the most wonderful and varied wildlife habitats on earth, with hundreds of different types of trees. Saving

them from destruction is one of the most important tasks facing the human race.

**FASTFACT:**
**In some places tropical rain forests are being destroyed at the rate of 100 acres every minute. In the time that it has taken you to read this page an area of rain forest as large as thirty football pitches will have disappeared.**

● **More trees, please**
Unlike rain forests, forests that are deliberately planted to produce a crop of timber are made up of just a few types of tree. They are carefully spaced out and planted in

blocks of single species. This allows them to grow quickly, all at the same speed. Then they can be harvested at the same time and the land replanted.

Many of the world's commercial forests are planted with conifers. These grow fast and when they are planted close together they produce tall, straight trunks that can be harvested after thirty to forty years.

Fast-growing conifers are sometimes called 'softwoods', because their rapid rate of growth tends to produce wood which is not as hard as that of the slower-growing broadleaved trees. Although the wood is light and soft it is still suitable for rough building timber and for producing paper pulp, used to produce newspapers, books and packaging.

Hardwoods, from broad-leaved trees, produce the best quality timber. Species like mahogany and ebony, which produce dense, beautifully coloured wood with a fine grain, are extremely valuable. Some of the world's most luxurious royal palaces have been built and decorated with mahogany panels. Today the best tropical hardwood forests have been ruthlessly exploited and the supply has almost run out.

## FASTFACTS:

**BIGGEST TREE:** *The giant sequoia called General Sherman, which weighs 2,000 tonnes and is said to be 3,000 years old, is claimed to be the largest living organism that has ever existed on earth.*

**TALLEST TREE IN BRITAIN:** *A grand fir in Strathclyde in Scotland is 63 metres high.*

**TALLEST CONIFER IN THE WORLD:** *A high coast redwood in California, over 110 metres tall.*

**TALLEST HARDWOOD TREE:** *A eucalyptus in Victoria, Australia – over 132 metres tall.*

**OLDEST TREE:** *Bristlecone pine from the mountains of Utah in the USA, over 5,000 years old.*

**TREE WITH THE LARGEST SPREAD OF BRANCHES:** *Probably the giant banyan tree. These produce roots that drop to the ground from their branches, so one tree can cover a vast area. There are many that cover an area as large as a football pitch.*

FASTEST GROWING TREE: *A tropical tree called Albizzia is known to be able to grow at a rate of 28 centimetres per day.*

LIGHTEST WOOD: *Balsa wood from Brazil is one of the world's lightest woods.*

HEAVIEST WOOD: *Ironwood is forty times heavier than balsa wood and does not float.*

# 14

. . . . . . . . . . . . . . . . . . . . . .

# PLANTS AND PEOPLE

When explorers from Europe sailed to the far corners of the earth they brought back strange and exotic plants. It soon became fashionable to grow these in gardens. Some of the explorers and collectors who mounted plant-hunting expeditions were amazing people. Besides being good at finding interesting plants, they needed to be strong and brave, because they had to live alone for months in jungles and forests. Often they were attacked by hostile natives and dangerous animals.

## FASTFACTS:
## SOME GREAT PLANT-HUNTERS

* John Tradescant sailed to America in 1637 and brought back Virginia creeper, which grows on the outside of many houses in England today.
* Captain William Dampier was born in 1652 and was a pirate who also collected flowers. He was the captain who marooned a sailor called Alexander Selkirk on a desert island. The famous book, *Robinson Crusoe* by Daniel Defoe, is based on Selkirk's experiences. Dampier discovered the bread-fruit tree (see page 80) and many other strange plants.
* Sir Joseph Banks sailed with Captain Cook to Australia

in 1768. Once, while plant-hunting in Tierra del Fuego in South America, he was trapped by a snowstorm and two of his colleagues died of exposure. The survivors were forced to eat vultures until they reached the safety of their ship. Banks later became the first Director of Kew Gardens and sent out many plant-collecting expeditions.

* Scotsman David Douglas began collecting plants in 1823 and visited the wildest parts of America in search of flowers. One of the trees that he brought back is the famous Douglas fir. He was killed by a bull while plant-hunting in Hawaii.

* Robert Fortune was one of the first plant-collectors to visit China. He went there during Queen Victoria's reign. He fought off several attacks by pirates on his plant-hunting expeditions.

* George Forrest collected plants in Tibet and China and narrowly escaped with his life when lamas attacked the Christian mission he was staying in. He collected many wonderful plants that gardeners grow today, including several gentians.

* Ernest Henry ('Chinese') Wilson, who died in 1930, brought back countless species of exotic plants from the Far East. Once, while trying to reach a specimen of the exotic regal lily, he almost lost a leg in an avalanche.

* Marianne North was an intrepid lady who travelled all over the world in search of rare plants. She painted pictures of them and often set up her easel in jungles, insect-infested swamps and on mountainsides, to capture plants at their best with her paint and brushes.

● The history makers
As explorers travelled across oceans and discovered new

continents, many countries grew wealthy by exploiting the valuable plants that they brought back. The battle to control sources of supply led to piracy, intrigue, wars, murder and mayhem.

● 'Hand over your mangoes, or I'll blast you out of the water!'

You have probably heard lots of stories of piracy. Usually they tell of the capture of exotic cargoes of Spanish dubloons, gold pieces-of-eight and precious silks, jewels and spices. But the most unusual cargo to be captured must surely have been the ship load of mangoes, that a Royal Navy sea captain seized in 1772.

Mangoes are wonderful fruits that are easy to grow in tropical countries. The French decided to introduce them on to the Caribbean island of Haiti (which was part of the French Empire) from an island in the Indian Ocean. At the time, France and England were at war (as they usually were in those days).

The French sea captain had the misfortune to meet a Royal Navy ship on the high seas. At first the British captain must have been disappointed not to find any gold coins aboard his prize, but he resisted the temptation to throw the mango trees overboard and carried them to the British island of Jamaica instead. Once they began to grow they were instantly popular with everyone. People picked them off the trees and threw away the large seeds inside. These germinated all over the island. Today mango is one of the commonest trees in Jamaica.

- **Mutiny on the *Bounty***

Less than twenty years after the capture of the French mangoes another sea drama, caused by a humble plant, took place. Bread-fruit triggered the most famous mutiny in history.

It grows in the South Sea Islands and produces an extremely nutritious fruit. So nutritious, in fact, that King George III commanded that it should be transported to the West Indies. He thought it would make a cheap source of food for the many slaves there.

In April 1789, Captain Bligh set sail from Tahiti aboard HMS *Bounty*. The ship was loaded with over 1,000 young bread-fruit trees planted in tubs and boxes. His destination was Jamaica.

As the days slipped by the crew grew more and more restless. Bligh had a bad temper and had his crew flogged for the slightest offence. He was also desperate to keep the precious bread-fruit trees alive. Although he gave his crew a tiny ration of water every day, he made sure that the plants got all the water they needed. The sailors grew restless. Led by Fletcher Christian, they began to mutter darkly among themselves. After three weeks of bad treatment they mutinied and cast Bligh and eighteen loyal members of his crew adrift in an open boat.

Bligh may have had an evil temper, but he was a good sailor and his skill in navigation guided him and his crew across 3,618 miles of open ocean to safety on the island of Timor. It was one of the most brilliant feats of seamanship in history.

Bligh was as stubborn as he was stern. When he returned to England in 1790, he planned another attempt to transport bread-fruit. He set sail in HMS *Providence* in 1792, and this time he succeeded in carrying the plants to the island of St Vincent in the West Indies.

As for Fletcher Christian and the mutineers, they sailed HMS *Bounty* back to Tahiti, set the ship on fire and settled on the island. Their descendants live there to this day.

● **King Cotton**
Slaves, like those whom the bread-fruits were intended to feed, were mostly used to grow and harvest plantation crops. The most important of these were cotton and sugar.

Cotton is made from the fibres which grow on the outside of the seeds of the cotton plant. Until the 1860s cotton was part of a large, evil trading triangle. The plants were mostly grown in the southern states of America. The cotton fibres were exported to England, where they were woven into cloth in the cotton mills of Lancashire. Meanwhile British ships scoured the coast of Africa in search of slaves, whom they transported to America and forced to work in the cotton plantations.

Slavery was abolished in England in 1807 but another

major link in this evil trade was not broken until 1861, when the American Civil War led to the defeat of the Confederate army and the freeing of the slaves.

### ● The not-so-sweet story of sugar

Sugar-cane is a large, thick-stemmed grass that is grown in tropical countries. Plantations in the West Indies once supplied almost all of the sugar for Europe, but today at least half of the sugar that we eat comes from another plant, sugar-beet.

Because it had to be transported long distances by sea, sugar from the tropical sugar-cane was very expensive and only the wealthy could afford to buy it.

During the Napoleonic Wars at the end of the seventeenth and beginning of the eighteenth centuries, the British Fleet prevented supplies of sugar from the West Indies reaching France. The Emperor Napoleon was livid and commanded his scientists to find a way of developing sugar-beet as an alternative crop.

Beet grew wild along the sea coast of Europe and scientists in Germany had already discovered that its roots contained sugar. Napoleon's scientists worked hard to breed plants with giant roots and therefore, more sugar.

Sugar-beet is now grown in very large quantities in Europe, while sugar-cane production has declined in many tropical parts of the world, often causing great hardship for peasant farmers.

### ● The tragic history of the chip

Next time you have chips with your dinner, remember the epic story of the potato.

In 1570 Spanish explorers brought potatoes to Europe from the foothills of the Andes in South America. It was the first link in a chain of events that led to the death of millions of people and the downfall of a government.

For almost 200 years the crop was grown mainly as a curiosity in Europe, because it only produced small tubers. But then varieties began to evolve that produced a much better crop of edible tubers. It quickly became a major source of food for the poor. In Ireland millions of people relied on this single crop, because they could not afford to pay the high prices for bread.

Then, in 1845 disaster struck. A tiny fungus called potato blight attacked the whole crop in Ireland. Potatoes rotted in the ground. For two years the harvest was wiped out. Famine set in and over a million people died. A million more fled to America as refugees, to start a new life.

### ● Rubber

Next time you are on a motorway journey, sitting in comfort as your car speeds along the tarmac, spare a thought for Henry Wickham. For it was he who played a key role in founding the great rubber plantations of the Far East, which supply much of the rubber that our car tyres are made from.

Rubber trees grow wild in the Brazilian jungle. The local Indians have known, for hundreds and perhaps thousands of years, how to wound the trees so that they bleed sticky latex. This is similar to the white, gooey liquid that oozes out of the cut stems of dandelions. When it solidifies, it turns into rubber. The Indians knew long ago how to make rubber bottles.

In the 1870s the British Government realized how valuable this versatile substance might be. Until that time latex was only extracted from the wild trees of the Brazilian jungle, but there were many places in the tropical parts of the British Empire where rubber might be grown. Collectors were despatched to bring back plants, but none survived the long sea voyage from South America.

Then Mr Wickham was sent from Kew Gardens. The Brazilian Government was reluctant to let rubber seeds out of the country, because they hoped to keep control of the world's rubber supply. But Wickham asked for the seeds as a present for Queen Victoria. The Brazilian governors were too polite to refuse, although they must have been a bit suspicious when he took 70,000 seeds to England as fast as his ship would carry him. But even so, only 3,000 seeds germinated when they arrived at Kew.

Meanwhile, gardeners in Ceylon (which is now called Sri Lanka), prepared nursery beds for the rubber seedlings. They were despatched from Kew Gardens aboard a fast steamship, in mini-greenhouses called Wardian Cases.

Long sea journeys had always made transporting live

plants very difficult. These cases, invented by Dr Nathaniel Ward, gave them plenty of protection from the harsh conditions at sea. Two thousand seedlings reached Ceylon, and more were sent to far-off Singapore. From Singapore a few seedlings were transported to a plantation in Malaya. There they founded a great rubber industry.

In Malaya the new crop was a massive success. When the automobile grew in popularity at the beginning of the twentieth century, designers began to look around for a material to replace the wooden carriage wheels that the first cars used. The old wooden wheels made automobiles into high-speed boneshakers, but rubber tyres proved ideal for a fast, smooth ride.

# 15

# THE WORLD'S MOST POISONOUS PLANTS

## ● Poison arrows

When the first explorers reached the dark jungles of South America, one of their greatest fears was the poison-tipped arrows of the Indians. The poison that they often used was curare, extracted from a jungle vine. When the needle-sharp arrows struck, death was an agonizing certainty. Curare is also known as strychnine and in modern times has been used as a medicinal drug.

## ● The executioner's potion

Hemlock is probably the most famous poisonous plant of all. In ancient Athens criminals who were sentenced to death were executed by being forced to drink hemlock juice. When Socrates, the famous philosopher, was condemned to death he took hemlock. Curious to the last, he described every symptom of the poison's effect as he died, so that his pupils could write them down.

## ● Foxglove – useful but deadly

Foxglove has been used in medicine for centuries. It acts as a heart stimulant, but it is very poisonous and should never be eaten.

• **Evil eye make-up**

Deadly nightshade's Latin scientific name is *belladonna*, which means 'beautiful lady.' This is because fine Italian ladies used to put juice from the berries in their eyes. It made the pupils, grow larger so that they looked wide-eyed and lovely. It was a very dangerous trick, because *belladonna* is extremely poisonous. Just one berry, which looks like a black cherry, could kill you. Eye specialists in hospitals still use an extract of deadly nightshade, called atropine, to make the pupils of eyes open wide; so that they can see into the eye itself.

• **Murder most foul**

Henbane is deadly. In *Hamlet*, one of Shakespeare's most famous plays, the King of Denmark was murdered by having henbane poured into his ear. Witches also used it in medieval magic. They spread henbane paste on their

heads and under their armpits. They believed it would make them have incredible dreams.

### ● The sleep of the dead

Thorn-apple came from America, but now grows all over Europe. It was often used in magic spells, to send people into deep sleeps, from which they sometimes never awoke. Hundreds of years ago Mexican indians used thorn-apple as an **anaesthetic** during painful operations, long before anaesthetics were used in Europe.

### ● Assassination by umbrella

Castor bean contains one of the deadliest of all poisons, called ricin. A few years ago a Bulgarian assassin murdered one of his fellow countrymen who was living in London. The murderer fired a tiny pellet coated with this poison into his victim's leg. He used a gun which was disguised as an umbrella! The pellet was so tiny that his victim hardly felt a thing, but there was enough poison on it to kill him.

## FASTFACTS:
### Some dangerous plants to avoid

* Laburnum . . . which has poisonous seeds.
* Yew . . . the seeds and leaves are extremely poisonous.
* Mezereon . . . has deadly purple berries.
* Water dropwort . . . many people have died from eating its tubers.
* Cuckoo-pint . . . its vivid red berries can be fatal.
* Wolfsbane . . . like monkshood, but with white flowers. Once used on the tip of arrows that were used to kill wolves.
* Lily of the Valley . . . even poisons the water in the vases that its flowers are placed in.
* Ragwort . . . poisons cattle. It is illegal to grow it in Britain.
* Holly . . . the glossy red fruits are poisonous.

### ● The witches' kitchen

Witches and wizards were notorious for poisoning their enemies. They were experts in finding the most deadly plants. One of their favourites was monkshood, whose flowers look like sinister, hooded monks' heads. Just a tiny portion of its root, craftily slipped into a drink, was enough to kill their victims.

### ● Mad dog's and mandrakes

When they were not murdering people, witches spent much of their time trying to find ways of becoming very rich and powerful. One of their favourite plants was mandrake, which grows in the mountains of Greece.

Wizards claimed that it had the power to open locked treasure chests, make people invisible and cure illnesses. So customers would pay a lot of money for magic potions with mandrake in them. It was a useful plant to have around, but there was one big problem to overcome before you could use it.

Mandrake roots grow in the shape of a human body, with underground branches that look like arms and legs. People believed that it grew like this because the seeds only germinated in ground where dead bodies had been buried. The roots were supposed to be full of evil spirits, that let out terrible, blood-curdling screams when the plant was wrenched from the soil and anyone who heard these screams would instantly go mad.

So if a wizard wanted to harvest a mandrake he needed a dog, a stick, a piece of string and some wax. He fixed the string to the dog's collar, tied the other end around the mandrake root, and stuffed the wax in his ears. Then he threw the stick and yelled 'Fetch!'

As the dog ran after the stick it wrenched the mandrake out of the ground. The wizard could not put any wax in the dog's ears, because then it would not hear its master shout 'Fetch.' Wizards do not seem to have worried about their dogs going mad!

● **Deadly bread**
There was a time when eating a slice of bread might make your toes drop off.

The reason for this is that rye, a plant similar to wheat and sometimes used to make bread, was often attacked by a fungus called ergot. This looks like a small black horn, about 2.5 centimetres long, which sticks out of the ear of grain. It is one of the most poisonous fungi in the world.

The symptoms of ergot poisoning were horrific. Victims said that to begin with it would make their flesh creep, as though swarms of ants were running around under the skin. Then their fingers and toes would go numb, slowly turn black and finally drop off. Sometimes people who ate ergot went mad and jumped out of windows, believing they could fly.

Ergot poisoning is *very* rare now, because modern bread-making techniques remove any ergot fungus that might get into the grain. So don't worry, you can eat up your crusts in complete safety!

● **Bringers of death and despair**
Although many plants produce valuable drugs that can improve our health and happiness, there are some which bring untold misery. These are the ones which produce substances that enslave those who use them, like tobacco, heroin and cocaine.

Such drugs often produce either a pleasant sensation of

well-being or strange dreams and hallucinations. But users become addicted. Once the plants get a grip, they quickly undermine the health of their victims. Sometimes addicts perform violent, evil acts to ensure their supply of drugs. The worst drugs can provoke deep depression, leading to suicide.

### ● The deadly weed

Tobacco is a legal stimulant which is now grown in vast quantities. It was introduced from South America by Spanish explorers. Tobacco contains nicotine, which is a powerful poison that has been used on a large scale to kill insects. Today, tobacco smokers are encouraged to stop using this dangerous plant product. It is known to cause many fatal illnesses, including heart disease and cancer.

### ● The assassins' drug

In the twelfth century an Arab known as Al-Hashan gathered around him a group of followers who lived by the evil cult of thugee – murdering innocent travellers and stealing their belongings. The thugs were men who were aggressive by nature and had become addicted to the resin of the Indian hemp plant, which gave its aggressive users false courage. Its Persian name, 'ashishin', gave rise to two other words: 'assassin', which describes the actions of many of the plants' users, and 'hashish', a more common name for the hemp plant. Hashish is also known by several other names, including marijuana and cannabis.

Hashish was once grown in lots of countries, including Britain, where the long, tough fibres of the stem were used for the production of rope. But it is the resin of the hashish plant that is by far its most valuable product.

Because its use is illegal in most countries, drug-dealers are able to charge very high prices for tiny amounts. Smuggling hashish is one part of the massive, world-wide drug trade that has destroyed the lives of hundreds of thousands of people.

### • Opium and cocaine

These two drugs, in their many forms, are by far the worst of the many illegal plant products sold in the backstreets and alleyways of the world.

Opium comes from the latex that oozes from cuts made in the capsule of opium poppies. It has been used to make several pain-killing drugs including morphine, named after Morpheus, the Greek god of sleep. Morphine was often used medically to relieve the suffering of injured people, and eased the pain of countless soldiers wounded in battle for centuries. But morphine is also used to make heroin, a drug that reduces human life to an endless cycle of pitiful craving and half-crazed sleep, relieved only by eventual death.

Cocaine comes from the leaves of the South American coca plant. Like many dangerous plant drugs, it has been used medically to the benefit of mankind. Dentists used it as an anaesthetic while they pulled out teeth, and it is still used in some surgical operations. It was even an ingredient of the popular drink Coca-Cola, until it was banned in 1904. By then its dangerous effects had been recognized.

Throughout the twentieth century a constant battle has been fought against the growers, manufacturers, smugglers and peddlers of dangerous plant drugs.

# 16
. . . . . . . . . . . . . . . . . . . . . . . .
# THE WORLD'S WORST WEEDS

Plants are beautiful and useful things, but sometimes they grow so fast and in such large numbers that they become a problem. Plants like this, that grow too well in places where we do not want them, are called weeds.

We humans have been fighting weeds since the dawn of civilization. It is a war which the plants are winning. No sooner has one green army been defeated than another springs up to take its place. Here are the short histories of the campaigns of some of the world's worst weeds.

● **A forest of fronds**
Bracken is a fern that grows almost everywhere in the world. Man has encouraged it to grow in many places and has often regretted it.

Ferns spread by producing tiny spores that grow on the underside of the feathery leaves. These spores can be carried for miles on the breeze. Once the spores germinate and a new fern grows it spreads by a creeping underground stem that can grow on and on for ever. In Yorkshire, in Northern England, bracken plants have been found that have been creeping in this way for a thousand years or more.

The bracken's secret weapons are its chemical defences. It is full of so many poisons that very few insects and other animals can eat it. When farm animals feed on it they often die. Bracken is steadily spreading and covers thousands of acres of land in England, Wales and Scotland. Farmers cut it, burn it and crush it. But it is still on the march, sending out clouds of poisonous spores every autumn. Creeping through the soil with its underground stems, nothing seems able to stop it. Now scientists plan to introduce to Britain a South African moth that they hope will eat it. This insect may be our best hope of defeating the green menace.

### • The vegetable armada

Water-hyacinth is a beautiful plant, with pretty spikes of pale blue and yellow flowers. It has large swollen leaf bases that act as bouyancy tanks and allow it to float on the surface of the water.

Water-hyacinth has floated down the tropical rivers of the world wherever it has been introduced, multiplying at a fantastic rate. Ten plants can cover an acre in eight months. It clogs dams, brings boats to a standstill and destroys fisheries. It has even spread into the flooded paddy-fields where rice is grown. There are plans to use it as food for animals, but it seems that nothing can stop its spread once it gets into waterways.

### • Unwanted guests

Many plants become weeds when they travel abroad. At home they can be perfectly well-behaved, but if they are taken to another country, where conditions suit them better, they can sometimes go berserk.

Take prickly-pear for example. This is a harmless cactus in its native Mexico, but when it was taken to Australia it behaved like it owned the country. It spread just about everywhere in a few decades and took over

## Making a fern-spore print

You can make a fern-spore print in the same way that you made a mushroom-spore print. Find a fern with spore cases under the fronds, just as they are about to burst. This usually happens towards the end of summer. Put the frond, spore-side down, on a sheet of white paper and leave it overnight. By morning the spores will have left a frond-shaped print.

FIND A FERN WITH SPORE CASES UNDER ITS FRONDS.

PLACE FERN, SPORE-SIDE DOWN ON A PIECE OF PAPER.

LEAVE OVERNIGHT – THE SPORES WILL LEAVE A FROND-SHAPED PRINT.

enormous areas of agricultural land before it was brought
under control. The Australians had to import a cactus-
eating moth from Argentina to destroy it.

The same story has been repeated in different parts of
the world. Dandelions were imported into Argentina
from Europe and spread like wildfire. European thistles,
ragweed and knapweed have been imported into the
United States and Canada and have tried to take over.
Once plants travel abroad, they often behave disgrace-
fully!

# 17

. . . . . . . . . . . . . . . . . . . . . . . . . .

# LIVING FOSSILS

Countless different types of plants have colonized the earth's surface since the first plants struggled to survive on land. Thousands of species have become extinct, making way for others that were more competitive or better adapted to changing climates.

What did the world's vegetation look like in the past? Fossils give us a clue, but there are a few plants – the living fossils – that occur as fossils *and* survive as living plants. They can reveal a glimpse of what plant-life might have looked like hundreds of thousands or even millions of years ago.

• **Ginkgo – going, going, almost gone**
160 million years ago Ginkgo, also known as the maidenhair tree, grew in many parts of the world, but until 1754 botanists believed that it only existed as fossils in the shape of beautiful, fan-shaped leaves in rocks. Then living maidenhair trees were discovered in monastry gardens in China, where cultivation had saved them from extinction. Today this elegant 'living fossil' is grown in parks and gardens all over Europe and North America and its future seems secure.

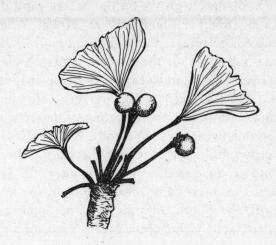

**FASTFACT:**
There are separate male and female Ginkgo trees, but only males are grown in parks. This is because the females produce fruit that smells disgusting!

• **Last minute reprieve for the dawn redwood**
Until 1945 everyone believed that this pretty tree, which looks like today's fir trees, had been extinct for thousands of years. Fossil impressions of its leaves were common in rocks, but no living tree had ever been seen. Then, in 1941 a Chinese botanist found a few trees that were about to be cut down for timber and he collected the seeds. Today the tree is grown in most of the world's botanic gardens and has returned from the brink of extinction, to show us how prehistoric forests might have looked.

• **Welwitschia – lone survivor from a lost world**
Welwitschia is one of the world's most bizarre and

mysterious plants. It grows on the barren sand dunes of the Namib Desert in South West Africa. When Welwitschia seeds germinate they produce two thick, leathery leaves that must last for the rest of the plant's life, which may be over a thousand years. The strap-shaped leaves are more than a metre wide and grow to almost 10 metres in length before the buffeting of desert winds and abrasive sands wear away the ends. New leaf-tissue constantly grows from the centre of the plant, where cones sprout and produce seeds at irregular intervals. The plant depends for its survival on moisture from sea mists that roll in off the South Atlantic Ocean. Some botanists believe that Welwitschia is the last survivor of a group of plants that were the ancestors of today's conifers and flowering plants, and has somehow survived the massive upheavals of geological history.

# 18

# PLANTS IN PERIL

Greed drives people to commit desperate crimes. Sometimes temptation comes from money, gold, jewels or art treasures. Sometimes it comes from exotic flowers.

- **Raiders of the last orchid**
These bizarre flowers, with their glowing colours, are designed to attract insects, but they also hold a great fascination for humans. For at least two hundred years orchid hunters have travelled to far-away places in search of rare and unusual varieties.

The discovery of rare orchids has been known to tempt even the most respectable botanists to dig them up in large numbers. Some species are now reduced to a few plants. In Britain the last lady's slipper orchid is guarded day and night against thieves.

Orchids are slow growers. The seeds need to find a special fungus that will help them grow before the seedlings will develop into full-sized plants. It takes many years for some types to flower. Rare species are being stolen at a faster rate than they can grow.

Today there are international treaties which are designed to stop the collection and exportation of rare plants. Customs officers search suspicious characters. But the best hope of survival for rare orchids comes from the research of botanists. They are learning how to grow the plants from seed. Once they can be produced cheaply and in large numbers in greenhouses, thieves will no longer be able to make a fortune stealing them from the wild.

But despite these developments in **conservation**, the trade in rare plants goes on. As orchid-collecting becomes more difficult some thieves are stealing cacti from America and spring bulbs from the Eastern Mediterranean instead.

FASTFACT:
The slipper orchids have curious, bucket-shaped pouches on the front of the flower and are especially threatened. In China the Golden Slipper of Yunnan grows on a single limestone mountain whose location is a closely guarded secret. Collectors will pay thousands of dollars for a single plant.

- Plants and pollution
Today pollution is a major threat to plants. It comes in many forms.

- Acid rain
Acid rain forms when sulphur dioxide gas rises into the atmosphere as coal is burned. The gas dissolves in the water droplets of clouds and falls to earth as an acid rain that is absorbed by leaves which often die. Millions of acres of forest in Europe and North America have been damaged in this way.

- Low-level ozone
This colourless, poisonous gas is formed from the reaction between car exhaust fumes and sunlight. It drifts out into the countryside from cities and causes severe damage to the leaves of wild plants and crops.

- Ultraviolet radiation
Ozone gas naturally occurs in the stratosphere, which begins about ten miles above the earth's surface. Here the gas absorbs harmful ultraviolet radiation. Pollutants escape into the stratosphere and break down the ozone layer, which in turn lets more harmful ultraviolet radiation through. Scientists have already detected damage to some plants.

## • Heavy metals

Plants can absorb heavy metals from the soil. Although they might not do the plants much harm, we are at risk if we eat them. Heavy metals like lead, from car exhaust fumes, and cadmium, from industrial processes, are very poisonous to animals.

## • Radioactivity

Many plants are very good at absorbing radioactivity. When the Chernobyl nuclear reactor in the Ukraine caught fire in 1986, a cloud of deadly radioactive gas drifted over Europe. Rain washed some of this into the soil in the mountains of Cumbria in Northern England, where plants absorbed it. Soon the sheep that grazed on the plants were contaminated with radioactivity and were no longer safe to eat. Scientists now know that radio-activity from the Chernobyl accident will be carried by affected plants for many decades.

## • Say goodbye to 40,000 species

No one knows for sure exactly how many species of plants there are on earth. In the jungles and in the seas there are many that have never been described. But what we do know is that in some places they are disappearing fast.

We use about 1,500 of them, to feed us or to provide medicines and other useful products. We know almost nothing about most of the others. Some may contain drugs that could save lives, others might grow in dry conditions and produce food for people who are suffering from famine. So far we have not had time to find out.

But now something terrible is happening. More and more land is being used for growing crops, grazing animals, building towns and factories and constructing roads. Because of this plant species are beginning to disappear at a frightening pace. Jungles, full of priceless plants, are being burned to make way for cattle ranches. Swamps, full of exotic insectivorous plants, are being drained to make way for prairies of wheat.

Somehow, we must find a way to provide the houses and food that people need without destroying all of these plants. We will need them in the future.

When plants become extinct, and the last individual of a species vanishes from the surface of the earth, it is gone for ever. That species can never return.

Botanists estimate that about 25,000 species of flowering plant are endangered and that 40,000 species could become extinct in the wild by the middle of the next century. The world will be a poorer place when that happens.

## FASTFACT:
**Some parts of the world are amazingly rich in different types of plant. On the slopes of Mount Makiliang, a single volcano in the Philippines, there are more types of plants than in the whole of Britain.**

● **Extinction on your window-ledge**
Many people grow a pretty plant called African violet on their window-ledge. Gardeners have bred dozens of different versions of this plant and they are sold in large numbers every year as houseplants. In its wild jungle home the African violet is in serious danger of extinction. It lives on steep, rocky slopes in the dense jungles of East Africa. There the forests are being felled, destroying its habitat. This is just one of hundreds of plants whose future is threatened by the destruction of tropical forests. The day may come when it only exists as a houseplant.

# 19

# INTO THE FUTURE

Imagine this. Suppose you were growing old, and suppose you cut off your finger, put it in a large test tube, fed it and kept it warm. And then, before your eyes it began to grow. First an arm, then a body, head and legs, until a new and perfect young copy of you had grown. Impossible, of course, and the kind of story that nightmares and horror films are made of.

But it is not impossible for plants. If you cut off parts of a plant they can often grow into new, perfect copies of the original. So you can make a begonia or an African violet leaf grow into a whole cluster of new plants. By cutting the spiky leaves off the top of a pineapple and potting them, they will eventually grow into a new plant, with a pineapple fruit sprouting from the middle.

So in this way some individual plants could live for ever. In the giant redwood groves of California new trees grow from the roots of their ancient parents. In the Wahiba Sands desert of Oman old thorn trees fall into the sand and new ones spring from their roots. In Scotland there are some clumps of fescue grass that may be thousands of years old, and they keep producing new plants around their edges.

Gardeners and farmers grow all sorts of plants by making exact copies of them. Scientists call these copies clones. The tubers of a potato can be planted to produce clones of the parent. When you look into a field of potatoes, just remember that every plant there is a perfect copy of one original parent.

## • Plants by the million

Scientists have learned how to make plants multiply themselves even faster. By taking a tiny piece of stem or root and feeding it with the right chemicals, while they keep it in ultra-clean conditions, they can make it produce dozens of buds. Each bud can be separated and multiplied in the same way again, to produce dozens more. If the scientists start with one bud, in two weeks they could have ten plants, in a month a 100, in six weeks a 1,000 and in three months a million. They call this technique micropropagation. If you buy a plant in a garden centre it may well have been grown by this method, starting life as a green blob in a test-tube.

With some plants you can go even further. Plants are made up of millions of microscopic cells. Almost all of these can grow into a complete new plant if they are treated in the correct way. The trick is to take a piece of leaf and soak it in chemicals called enzymes. They make the cells separate from one another. Then they are grown in warm, clean conditions with plenty of nutrients. Soon, each cell will divide to make a small group of cells. Then each of these will grow into a new plant.

The latest trick that scientists have learned is to combine cells from different plants, so that the new 'super cell' grows into a plant that has features of both parents. In this way they have combined cells of potatoes and tomatoes to make a plant that looks a bit like both. Is it a pomato or a totato? Who knows?

### • The bottomless botanical oil well

Oil that we burn in cars and power stations was formed millions of years ago, when plants decayed and were buried. Sooner or later these fossil supplies of energy will run out. The search is on for new sources of fuel.

Plants are a wonderful source of energy, because they use raw materials that are renewed every day. They use sunlight to convert water and carbon dioxide to sugars and then use these to make other substances, including oil. Plants are a clean source of energy that could last for ever if we use it well.

To get an idea of the variety of plant oils, visit your local supermarket. There you will find oils that are used for cooking, extracted from seeds of sunflower, olives, oilseed rape, sesame, grapeseed, walnuts, corn, ground-nuts and soybeans. These are all products of sunshine, carbon dioxide and water, combined and processed by plants in farmers' fields.

They are just a few of the plant oils available. Cotton seeds, left over once the cotton fibres have been removed, are crushed to extract large quantities of valuable oil. Linseed produces a slow-drying oil which is used in

making paints and linoleum for floor coverings. Chemists can modify plant oils for a wide range of uses, from lubricating moving parts on space vehicles to making cosmetics.

Another potential use of vegetable oils is to power automobiles. Cars have already been built which will run on a bottle of sunflower oil from the supermarket shelf!

### ● Sunshine power

If you add yeast to a watery solution of sugar and leave it in a cool, dark place the process of fermentation begins. Bubbles of carbon dioxide gas rise to the surface and the yeast makes alcohol.

If this process is carried out on a grand scale, using tonnes of sugar-cane, large amounts of alcohol can be produced and extracted. This technique is already used in countries like the Philippines and Brazil to provide alcohol fuel for cars, to replace the petrol made from underground oil reserves. Recently scientists have devised techniques for turning wood into alcohol, so eventually we may be able to replace oil with energy captured from sunlight by forests.

### ● New plants for old

Plants can provide all of our basic needs – food, clothes, medicine, warmth and shelter – but scientists are always looking for new and better ways to use them.

Sometimes they hunt for new plants in remote jungles, sometimes they select the best varieties of existing plants. Plant breeders, for example, often try to select wheat plants with more seeds or vegetables with larger roots or leaves. The seeds of garden peas are at least four times bigger than wild peas because we have carefully selected larger ones, to increase our supply of food.

But recently scientists have made an astonishing break-through which could increase the value of plants even more.

It all started in 1866 when a monk called Gregor Mendel began to grow peas in his garden in a monastry in Brno, in what is now Czechoslovakia. He discovered that the characteristcics of plants and all other living things are controlled by particles inside cells called genes.

Genes control how tall a plant will be, the colour of its flowers and every other characteristic that you can think of. The colour of your eyes, skin, hair and all your other features are controlled by the genes in the cells that make up your body.

For almost a hundred years scientists puzzled over how genes worked, until in 1953 two researchers at Cambridge University cracked their secret chemical code. The scientists were called Jim Watson and Francis Crick and together they discovered that every cell contains a sub-stance called DNA, which is a kind of chemical code.

It soon occurred to scientists that if they could under-stand the code and change it, they could change the genes in cells and change the way that plants and animals grow.

And now they have done just that! Scientists can take genes and transfer them from one plant to another, or even between animals and plants. They call the process genetic engineering. Here are some examples of ways that it has already been used.

● **Frost resistant tomatoes**
Many foods can be frozen and stored until they are needed, but ice ruins tomatoes. If you put them in a deep freeze, they turn to a nasty, squelchy mess when they

thaw out. But genes from a flatfish in the arctic might change all that.

These fish swim in waters that are so cold they would freeze to death if it was not for the fact that their blood contains special proteins that protect them from the cold. Genetic engineers have managed to transfer the genes that make the anti-freeze protein from the flatfish into a tomato plant. The frost resistant tomato might soon be here.

### ● Plants that eat pollutants

Pollution is one of the world's worst problems and cleaning up the mess left by industry is often very difficult. But plants might come to the rescue.

In our blood we have substances called antibodies, which attack anything nasty that gets into our bloodstream. Antibodies are chemicals that grab viruses or poisonous substances and hang on tight to them or destroy them, so that they cannot do us any harm.

Genetic engineers have taken the genes for antibodies from animals and put them into plants. They hope the plants will then make antibodies that will grab poisonous metals or toxic chemicals and hold them in the plant. The plants could then be harvested and the dangerous chemicals extracted and destroyed.

### ● Bean genes beat bugs

Every year millions of tonnes of the world's food, which is desperately needed by starving people, is eaten by insects. To save our crops from destruction we have to treat them with poisonous sprays which kill insects but often harm us and our environment too. We can sometimes breed crops that pests do not like but it is a very slow process. Meanwhile, the shortage of food in many countries becomes more desperate every day.

Some years ago scientists in Nigeria discovered a variety of African pea, called cowpea, which contains a substance that insects do not like. Scientists at Durham University in England identified the substance and located the gene which makes it. This can now be very quickly transferred to all sorts of crop plants. So far, it seems that caterpillars and bugs cannot eat the leaves that contain the bean genes, so they look elsewhere for something to eat. Genetically engineered crops that do not need to be sprayed with deadly chemicals to control pests now seem to be just around the corner.

Genetic engineering is a very new technique. No one is sure whether there are hidden dangers in moving genes around in this way. But it does seem that the new technology could help us to use plants more efficiently so that future generations will be able to say – 'That's Plantastic.'

# GLOSSARY

. . . . . . . . . . . . . . . . . . . . . . . . .

**Anaesthetic**
Chemical substances that make people unconscious, so that they cannot feel pain. Dentists use anaesthetics when they pull out teeth. Surgeons use them when they perform operations on sick people in hospitals.

**Antibiotic**
Chemicals that kill **bacteria** and other living organisms which attack people and cause disease.

**Bacteria**
Tiny, primitive organisms made up of single cells, that can multiply with incredible speed. Some bacteria, like Salmonella which contaminates food, are harmful. Some serious diseases, like diphtheria and typhoid, are caused by bacteria. Others are harmless or even useful, like the bacteria that are used to make yoghurt.

**Carbon dioxide**
This is the gas which is made when carbon burns in oxygen. Its chemical formula is $CO_2$. Plants use it to make sugars, so it is essential for their growth.

**Carnivorous**
The word used to describe organisms that eat the flesh of animals. Lions are carnivorous. So are Venus fly-traps.

**Cells**
All living organisms are made of cells. A typical plant cell

is about one tenth of a millimetre across – too small to see with the naked eye.

## Chlorophyll

This is the green pigment in plant cells. It traps energy from sunlight and uses this to convert carbon dioxide and water into sugars.

## Conservation

Wild plants and animals are often endangered by the activities of people. Farming, building towns and roads, cutting down forests and the pollution from industries can all harm wildlife. Conservation is the word used for the work that people do to protect wildlife from these dangers.

## Digest

Means to dissolve. We digest our food by dissolving it with **enzymes** inside our bodies, breaking it down into a form that we can use as fuel to keep our bodies healthy.

## Environment

The conditions that living organisms exist in. These can be a combination of temperature, moisture, wind, sunshine, soil conditions and levels of pollution.

## Enzymes

These are chemicals that break down dead plants and animals into simpler chemicals that other animals or plants can use for growth. We have enzymes in our stomachs that break down meat and vegetables into chemicals that our bodies can use for growth and energy.

## Evolution

The way in which plants and animals gradually change

over long periods of time, so that they can survive in a changing **environment**.

### Fermentation

This happens when enzymes break down sugar, turning it into alcohol and carbon dioxide gas. This is how alcoholic drinks like beer and wines are made.

### Germinate

Seeds germinate when they get wet. This makes their cells swell up, so that the seed coat bursts. Then the root and the shoot of the baby plant inside push their way out. They use up stored food reserves until they are strong enough to survive on their own.

### Global-warming

An increase in average temperatures, measured over the course of a year, which is taking place all over the planet, because the greenhouse effect is getting stronger.

### Greenhouse effect

When the sun's rays strike the earth's surface it heats up. The earth releases this heat again but some of it is trapped by gases in the atmosphere, which prevents the heat from escaping back into outer space. This is the greenhouse effect, which keeps the earth warm. Carbon dioxide is one of the greenhouse gases which is increasing in the atmosphere, because we are burning large amounts of oil and coal. This is making the greenhouse effect stronger, so **global-warming** is taking place.

### Gravity

This is the force that pulls objects towards the centre of the earth and stops them floating off into space.

# Habitat

This is the name given to the type of ecosystem that a plant or animal is usually found in. The habitat of buttercups is a meadow and the habitat of bluebells is a woodland.

# Hyphae

Mushrooms and toadstools are made of tiny threads called hyphae, that grow by dissolving their way through the substances that they grow on.

# Liverwort

The most primitive type of land plant. The simplest liverworts grow as a flat, green ribbon that branches over the soil surface.

# Molecule

All gases, solids and liquids are made of countless tiny molecules, which are too small to see, even with a microscope. Molecules are made when smaller particles, called atoms, combine. So when two atoms of hydrogen gas (chemical symbol H) combine with one atom of oxygen (chemical symbol O), a molecule of water is formed (chemical symbol $H_2O$).

# Nitrogen

About eighty per cent of the atmosphere is made of nitrogen gas (chemical symbol N). Nitrogen is essential for plant growth but they cannot use it directly. First it must combine with oxygen, to make nitrate molecules, or with hydrogen, to form ammonia molecules, which dissolve in water and can be absorbed and used by plants.

## Nutrients
Substances that plants must use for growth. These include nitrogen and minerals such as iron (chemical symbol Fe), potassium (chemical symbol K) and phosphorous (chemical symbol P).

## Oxygen
Oxygen is the gas that we breath, which keeps us alive. Its chemical symbol is O and the chemical formula for oxygen is $O_2$. It is made by plants, which release it into the atmosphere when they carry out **photosynthesis**.

## Parasite
Parasites are plants and animals that live on other, living plants and animals. They usually kill them slowly.

## Pheromones
These are chemical scents that some insects use to communicate with each other. Sometimes they are released by female moths, so that male moths can find them in the dark. Ants leave a trail of pheromones between food sources and their nest, so other ants can follow it to find the food.

## Photosynthesis
This is the chemical reaction that plants use to convert carbon dioxide from the atmosphere and water from the soil into sugars that they can use for growth. Plants use the green pigment in their leaves, called **chlorophyll**, to capture the energy from sunlight, which they then use for photosynthesis.

## Pollen
Tiny cells, like dust, that are released from flowers and which fertilize the eggs, or ovules, in other flowers.

Pollen is often carried in the wind or by insects, like bees and butterflies, which visit flowers.

## Pollination
This is the process of transferring pollen from the stamens of a flower, where it is made, to the sticky stigma, where it begins to grow down towards the eggs.

## Proteins
These are very complicated molecules, made of carbon, hydrogen, oxygen and nitrogen, that are part of the cells of all living organisms, where they are essential for growth and repair. Proteins are often stored in seeds and are used up by the seedling when the seed **germinates**.

## Radioactive
Radioactive elements change from one form to another as time passes, giving out radioactivity as they change. Radioactivity is often dangerous for humans. Too much of it can kill you, but it also has important uses in medicine.

## Species
This is the general word used by biologists when they talk about different types of plants and animals. Daisies, buttercups and dandelions are all different species of flower, because each has characteristics that makes it different from other similar flowers.

## Spore
Some plants, like mosses and ferns, grow from minute spores that are much smaller and simpler than seeds. Spores blow long distances in the wind, so new ferns and mosses can turn up almost anywhere that the soil is wet enough for germination. All fungi produce spores.

### Stamen
The part of the plant where pollen is made.

### Starch
An important material that plants store in their cells. It is made from the sugar that plants make from carbon dioxide and water.

### Stigma
The sticky surface in a flower where pollen begins to grow. The pollen sends out a fine tube that grows downwards, through the flower, to the egg cells.

### Stomata
Tiny pores in the surface of leaves, which let carbon dioxide in and let oxygen and water vapour escape.

### Sulphur
Sulphur (chemical symbol S) is often found in coal. When this is burned in power stations the sulphur combines with oxygen gas to form sulphur dioxide gas (chemical symbol $SO_2$). When this rises into the air it dissolves in raindrops and falls to earth as acid rain.

### Tubers
These are either swollen stems or swollen roots, where plants store starch for future use.

# INDEX